PORTRAIT
of an
ANOREXIC

PORTRAIT
of an
ANOREXIC
A Mother and Daughter's Story

Maureen Ardell
Corry-Ann Ardell

Flight Press
Vancouver

*To Lorna
and
to Dale*

Flight Press
2-3630 West Broadway
Vancouver, B.C., Canada V6R 2B7

Canadian Cataloguing in Publication Data

Ardell, Maureen, 1966-
  Portrait of an anorexic

ISBN 0-919843-02-6

1. Ardell, Maureen, 1966-   2. Anorexia nervosa—
Patients—Biography. I. Ardell, Corry-Ann, 1939-
II. Title.
RC552.A5A72 1985   616.85'2   C85-091003-X

Designed by Barbara Hodgson
Typeset by Baseline Type & Graphics Cooperative
Printed in Canada by D.W. Friesen & Sons Ltd.

CONTENTS

PREFACE

In the spring of 1983, Maureen was admitted to Shaughnessy Hospital in Vancouver for the treatment of anorexia nervosa. One of our biggest worries at the time was how she could keep up with her schoolwork. Her English teacher suggested she keep a journal as part of her course work. After Maureen was released from the hospital, we gave the journal to a close relative who works in publishing and asked her if she thought it might have some value for other young people. She encouraged us to have the journal published, especially since there seemed to be only a few personal accounts by anorexics available. The books we had seen were either medical descriptions of the illness or personal stories of a somewhat sensational nature.

We also thought it might be beneficial to include the mother's point of view, and Corry-Ann began to write down some of her thoughts and feelings. Although the story is mainly Maureen's, we have included an opening section describing Corry-Ann's experiences dealing with the pain and grief of having a daughter who is anorexic. Each of us has also written an epilogue describing the victories we have won and the struggles that have remained since Maureen was released from the hospital. We hope this dual approach might be of some help and encouragement both to anorexics and to their families.

We are grateful to so many for their help and encouragement—Dan Fossey, who tried to mark Maureen's journal as a school assignment; dear Auntie Margie, who started the ball rolling; Judy Hiron, who typed the first draft of the manuscript several mornings before work; and all our friends and relatives who responded with enthusiasm to the idea of a book about our experiences. And we want to thank our publisher, Nancy Flight—whom we call the dentist because getting this manuscript out of us was like pulling teeth — for her patience and understanding.

We have tried to be honest about our own experiences and to share our deepest emotions. We hope that by doing so we might help others avoid some suffering or gain a little insight into anorexia nervosa.

MOTHER

It was a spring afternoon, and we were at a baby shower. Warm sunshine flooded the room. The table was piled with pastel-colored gifts amid a profusion of paper and ribbons. I was sitting on the floor, crowded together with some close friends, talking and laughing. I was enjoying myself, and I felt especially happy for my young friend who had recently borne her first child.

But when my glance fell on my own fourteen-year-old daughter, I felt a stab. Maureen was so pale. Her eyes were darkly shadowed and had no sparkle. Her long blond hair was limp and lifeless. She had become so thin in the past few months that she seemed lost inside her jeans and sweater. Usually she liked to help serve the refreshments, but today she just sat quietly on the floor beside me, not even bothering to join in the laughter.

I reminded myself that the doctor had checked her over and said that she was healthy enough, she just needed to eat more. But why did she have trouble eating? She always said that she had no appetite.

I turned to the friend sitting closest to me. Katherine was a motherly woman who had raised six children. I wondered if she had ever worried about a thin child who didn't have much appetite.

"I'm so worried about Maureen," I murmured to her so that Maureen wouldn't hear. Perhaps I thought that sharing my worry would dissipate some of it. Or perhaps I just wanted reassurance, to be told that I had nothing to worry about. Her reply was like a slap in the face.

"Maureen looks like a cadaver," she said coldly.

I couldn't speak. I turned away from her judgmental, accusing face. My first concern was for Maureen, but she didn't seem to have heard what Katherine had said. As Maureen smiled up at me, I had to look away from her too, blinking back the tears.

1

"I think I'll get myself a coffee," I said as I rose to my feet. "I'll be right back."

I felt a confusion of emotions as I walked away. Anger that someone I considered a friend should speak so callously. Shock at her lack of tact. Fear that there was something seriously wrong with Maureen. Helplessness. What could I do about a girl so thin that she was compared to a cadaver?

I had heard of anorexia nervosa, of course. But, to me, anorexia nervosa suggested an extremely unbalanced mind, and Maureen was a sensible, reasonable girl. I also knew that anorexics consider themselves fat even when other people tell them they look like skeletons. But Maureen told me that she knew she was too thin. It hurt her when people referred to her as skinny. That's one of the reasons I was upset by what Katherine said. How would Maureen have felt if she had heard such an unkind comment?

I also knew that emotional problems often arose in families that were not united and loving. But my husband Dale and I had made a happy, healthy family life our highest priority. Surely only children from families torn by friction and strife would be forced to seek refuge in such sick behavior.

So even though I had heard of anorexia nervosa, and even though I was shocked by my friend's description of Maureen, I still didn't believe that she was deliberately refusing to eat enough to keep her weight normal. Perhaps if Katherine had tried to discuss my feelings and worries with me and had told me that she thought I had good reason to worry about Maureen, I wouldn't have become defensive and might have faced the problem sooner. But her cruel comment only made me more confused. I would think to myself, "Maureen looks much too thin, but the doctor says she's not sick. She says she is trying to eat. I see her eating. I know she doesn't make herself vomit. What could be wrong with her? It must be a passing phase. Surely she'll grow out of it. I'll just give her a little more time. She'll be OK."

Then I would think, "Maybe she's so thin because she's working too hard at her schoolwork. Ever since she started grade nine she's been overly serious about her marks. She's so much like her father that way—always striving to do better. If I could only get her to relax more and, more important, to eat more. People like Katherine just don't understand. Does she think I don't know that Maureen is too thin? What can I do? How did this happen?

2

Looking at my hollow-eyed daughter, I found it hard to believe she was the same Maureen I had cuddled as an infant. She had been a healthy, beautiful baby — round, bouncy, and lovable. The babysitter nicknamed her Chubby Chicken. She appealed to everyone with her sweet smile, yellow hair, pink cheeks, and blue eyes.

Even then, though, she was high-strung. Sweet-natured though she was, she was scared of loud noises and new experiences. Having her picture taken with a flash camera was an ordeal for her. She would cower in fright, her little face contorted with emotion. I still have a snapshot of her when she was two or three years old, her chubby baby hands pressed to her cheeks and her eyes wide with apprehension. I am crouched in the background, smiling reassurance, my hand on her shoulder.

She was also frightened of the vacuum cleaner and the lawn mower. When someone was cutting the lawn, Maureen would suddenly disappear. Later, I would find her hiding in the bedroom with her pillow over her head. She never made a fuss or demanded attention, but I would always go to her and try to soothe her fears. I never thought that her fears were abnormal but chalked them up as evidence that every human being is different.

Maureen was different from most children in another way. If she skinned her knee and came to me for sympathy, a few hugs and kisses were rarely enough, as they had been for her older sister, DaleAnn. Maureen needed protracted sessions of soothing before she was ready to give up her tears. She wasn't easily distracted from her unhappiness, but fortunately she was seldom sad and I was willing to spend the extra few minutes with her when she needed them.

She went off to school a sturdy, happy child and became popular with the other kids. There was always some child ringing the doorbell: "Can Maureen come out to play?"

But she did worry me sometimes. "I'm scared to go to school today," she would say. "We are going to learn to print P. I can't do P; it's too hard." I was puzzled that she should feel so insecure, but I always reassured her and tried to build her confidence.

Maureen was an unusually good girl. Other people noticed too. One of her little friends sighed and asked her mother, "Why isn't Maureen ever bad?"

Dale and I were firm and consistent with our discipline, and she knew what behavior we expected of her. She was very rarely disobedient. DaleAnn was also obedient, but occasionally she would push us just to see if we had changed our minds and she might get away with something for once. But Maureen never seemed to want, or need, to test the limits of our patience. Bedtime was never a hassle; she never took another child's toy or hit another child. I was happy that Maureen was such an easy child to raise, but sometimes I would wonder why she was so serious and so sensitive.

Dale often commented that Maureen was going to have to toughen up somehow before she grew up. She was exceptionally soft-hearted. Even reading stories about animals, she'd shake her head sadly and say, "Poor little bunny. He doesn't get any supper."

"But he probably wasn't hungry. He'll get some supper later."

"I know. But he is still a poor little bunny."

For the most part, Maureen's elementary school years were happy for her — playing with her many friends, riding her bike with her blond braids flying, learning to play the piano and the autoharp, finding out she was a good singer and a fast runner. But when it was time to go off to junior high school, Maureen didn't find life so pleasant. Some of the girls she had been friends with in elementary school drifted off to new friendships and then dropped those and picked up different ones again. This shifting of friends was often accompanied by teasing, gossip, and snubs. Maureen asked me why the girls had to be so mean, and all I could say was that I remembered girls acting the same way when I was in grade eight and that soon she would find other, more loyal friends.

She did make other friends, including a girl who was very overweight. One day as Maureen and her new friend walked through the hallway at school, an older boy commented loud enough for all to hear, "Look! A dog and a cow." Maureen laughed when she told me, but I knew she was hurt. I tried to make light of the episode, but Maureen began to refer to her appearance more often, saying, "I hate my hairstyle," or "I've got such a round face."

Sometime before starting grade nine, Maureen embarked on a self-improvement course. She didn't say anything to anyone, but she decided she was going to work hard to improve her appearance and to become a top student.

Her bangs grew out enough that she could fasten them back smoothly, revealing her little oval face, shapely forehead, and lovely hairline. Her long blond hair fell over her shoulders now, and she kept it clean and shining. She lost a few pounds by skipping desserts

4

and snacks, and she got some stylish new jeans for school in September. On the first day of grade nine, she went off to school looking great and feeling pleased with herself.

One of Maureen's teachers that year took a special interest in her. He told her she was an unusual student, mature and deep. She spent long hours talking with him in his office. He had very high standards for his students and she couldn't bear to disappoint him in any way. She began to work harder than she ever had before. She felt nervous that she might fail her mentor, but she was pleased and proud that someone thought she was an especially good student. She would spend almost all her time at home in her bedroom with her books. When we insisted that she come with us on some family outing, she resented being taken away from her studies. Dale and I frequently tried to cajole her into joining her sister or her friends in some recreational activity, but she always had a report that was due or some pressing assignment or exam coming up.

School work [handwritten marginal note]

She was still on the diet she had started during the summer before grade nine. We hadn't forbidden her to diet because she did tend to be chubby and she was such a great after-school snacker. She used to put away two peanut butter sandwiches before supper and still have room for a good meal and dessert. So we agreed that I would help her lose a few pounds by keeping celery and carrots on hand. We told her that she had to eat balanced meals and that she couldn't skip meals at all. She readily agreed.

Maureen proved to be an excellent dieter. She became knowledgeable about nutrition and showed admirable self-control. She would measure out exactly half a teaspoon of butter for her whole-wheat toast. She never used jam, of course; nor did she seem to miss it. When the rest of us had a piece of cake, she would have a piece of fruit. She never seemed to suffer from any feelings of self-pity if I served something like strawberry shortcake, but she would cheerfully prepare herself a dish of plain strawberries with a little of her daily milk allowance poured over it. She often said such things as, "I need one more bread serving today," or "I'll have half a banana before I go to bed. I haven't had enough fruit today."

Maureen didn't like to eat out because it was hard for her to control what she ate. She preferred to eat at McDonald's, where she could order a plain hamburger and a diet pop. Then she would allow herself an ice cream cone for dessert.

She had several booklets that listed the calorie count of various foods, and she seemed to have them all memorized. Just mention a food and she would tell you how many calories it had. She carried the booklets around with her in her purse and would carefully consult them when planning her meals.

Maureen's favorite snack was a raw carrot, and she would often nibble on one while she was studying. After a while she began eating so many carrots that her hands and feet and even her face took on a decidedly orange cast. At that point I really became concerned and told her she was overdoing her diet.

Mealtimes were becoming unpleasant too. Maureen would arrange her cutlery precisely and spread her paper napkin on her lap. Then she would take small amounts of food and spread them over her plate. Watching her made me uncomfortable, and I always felt tense beause Dale would often make some critical remark about her eating habits. Maureen would not respond but would sit there in sullen silence.

By this time, Dale and I were quite worried about Maureen. It was obvious that she had lost too much weight. Her clothes were too loose, and she seemed to be trying to hide herself in layers of clothing. Each week her face looked thinner and her eyes seemed larger.

One evening, as Maureen cut off small bites of food and slowly nibbled at them, Dale decided that he had had enough.

"Maureen, that's ridiculous. I want you to take more food. You are much too thin."

Maureen didn't change the expression on her face. "I'm not hungry tonight."

"Why not? Did you have a snack before supper?"

"No."

"Then why aren't you hungry?"

"I don't know. I don't feel very well today."

"Well, no wonder you don't feel very well! You don't look well either. I don't think you are eating enough. Here, have some more potatoes."

Maureen took the bowl and helped herself to a little more of the potatoes. She ate them slowly and grimly. She was silent for the remainder of the meal, and so were the rest of us.

I felt sorry for her. She did seem to be trying. And I didn't like the idea of telling a fourteen-year-old what and how much to eat. I knew

6

it was time for her to start making some of her own decisions, and what better place to start than with her food? I had never approved of parents who forced their children to eat and made such a fuss that they ended up with a real eating problem. I also thought that forcing her to eat when she didn't want to might cause her to rebel and only make things worse. So I just held my breath and hoped for the best. Perhaps if she had tried to eat only a lettuce leaf for supper, or if I had seen her actually skip a meal, I would have faced the fact that Maureen had a serious eating problem sooner. I found out later that most of the lunches I saw her pack—a sandwich and fresh fruit and vegetables—ended up in the garbage, and that a good part of the meals she put on her plate went into the napkin on her lap and then into the garbage when she cleared the table.

Maureen insisted that she knew she was thin enough and that she was earnestly trying to put on a little weight. Somehow, she said, she just couldn't seem to do it. She felt full all the time and never seemed to get hungry.

Perhaps there was something physically wrong with her, I thought. Maybe some insidious illness was wearing her down. Dale and I agreed that it was time to check things out with our family doctor.

I told the doctor that we were worried because Maureen had lost a few pounds recently and now seemed to be too thin and without any appetite. After weighing her, he said that she was a few pounds underweight and should try to beef up her diet. He said that it was up to her and that I should not interfere or try to force her to eat. In retrospect, I'm sure he thought she was a finicky eater with a hovering mom. But Maureen had always been a good eater up until this time.

I was relieved that our doctor seemed to take Maureen's problem so lightly, but she still didn't look well and people began to comment on how thin she had become. The school counselor phoned to say that she and some of the teachers were concerned about Maureen's health. I felt so ashamed! No other teacher or counselor had ever found it necessary to phone us about a problem. Surely they didn't think we hadn't noticed Maureen didn't look well! I assured the counselor that Dale and I were aware of the problem, and I explained that I had taken Maureen to the doctor recently and that he hadn't found any physical ailment. We discussed the fact that Maureen was working too hard at her schoolwork, but the counselor had no practical suggestions for remedying the problem.

My sister had been worried about Maureen for some time as well, and her comments and questions were bothering me. What could I tell her when I had no answers myself? Then one day she asked me again, "Why is Maureen so thin? Why can't you get her to eat more? She looks terrible!"

"I don't know. She is trying to eat more lately. She isn't skipping any meals, you know. It's just that she's never very hungry."

My sister looked at me in disgust and exploded in anger. "You are just standing by while your daughter literally fades away in front of your eyes!"

"I just took her to the doctor!" I defended myself.

"Well, take her again! There is something wrong with her. You've got to *do* something!"

I felt so powerless and frustrated. I had enough of a burden worrying about Maureen's weight, but that she was thin was only part of my worry. Her whole personality had changed since she had entered grade nine. I thought her problem was that she was obsessed with schoolwork to the point that she could no longer enjoy life, including eating. Now teachers, relatives, and friends seemed to be accusing me of being a bad mother because Maureen was too thin. That was especially hard for me to take. I was not very sure of myself in most areas, but I knew I was a good mother. I thought part of being a good mother was to help Maureen with her fears and worries and not to rush around frantically discussing her problems with everyone or whining that I couldn't handle her.

I did take her to another doctor for an unrelated reason and mentioned in passing that we were worried about her because she was so thin and yet had trouble eating enough. He recommended that she have a milkshake every night before bed. Maureen agreed to try, and every night we'd make a concoction of milk, egg, and a banana in the blender. She would have a hard time getting it down, and sometimes couldn't finish it, but she seemed to be trying.

It was about this time that we watched the television movie *The Best Little Girl in the World*. The title made me nervous because Maureen had always been such a good girl. I firmly resolved to be honest with myself as I watched it. Was there a resemblance between the girl in the story and Maureen?

After watching the show, I was convinced that Maureen couldn't be suffering from anorexia nervosa. The girl in the movie was

8

obviously from a sick and hypocritical family. She and her parents acted as if they were close and loving in public, but in private they screamed and cursed at each other. The parents held her down and tried to force food into her mouth. She retaliated by throwing up. The vomiting seemed to be the focus of the disease, and, since I was sure that Maureen had never made herself vomit, I thought she could not be anorexic. And certainly we never treated each other with the lack of respect, even animosity, that this family displayed.

Maureen continued to work hard at school and on her homework. Her report cards showed the result of her hard work and determination. She received straight A's in every class, and at the end of the year she was awarded a huge trophy for being the best student in grade nine. But it was a very thin and pale girl who accepted that trophy. Proud though I was, I wondered if she had sacrificed too much to achieve her goal. Since starting grade nine she had been working for the trophy she now held in her arms. Late nights of studying, worrying herself sick over exams, writing elaborate reports and essays had all paid off. But she had never had any time for fun. Perhaps all that work and worry had affected her appetite. Looking back over the year, I wondered if we should ever have let her start a diet in the first place.

Our family was suffering from other problems beside Maureen's health at this time. Dale had accepted a job in Cranbrook, so we knew we'd be leaving Kamloops as soon as school was out. We sold our house at the end of March, with occupancy date at the end of June. So for three months Dale was in Cranbrook without us, starting his new job and building our new house. Then the blow fell. The people who had bought our house said they had changed their minds. The papers were signed, the bank financing arranged, and our new house half-built. Now we had to get a lawyer, rearrange the financing, and try to resell the house. It was a worrisome time, and we all felt a tremendous strain.

We didn't resell the Kamloops house for another year, but at this point at least our Cranbrook house was almost finished. Dale thought that the girls and I could help speed things up and we could be together sooner if we would paint the inside of the house. It was a big job, but, dressed in old clothes and armed with rollers and paint trays, we began our work.

We were staying with friends, sleeping in strange beds, eating

9

different food, and working hard all day. Maureen would push herself grimly for a couple of hours and then have to stretch herself out on the paint-splattered floor, exhausted, until she could regain some strength. I could see that she was eating less than ever—she just nibbled at things and pushed the food around her plate while she supported her head with her hand. For several nights, too, she had very little sleep. She went to bed early every night feeling very tired from the day's work, but she had trouble sleeping. In the morning she would come downstairs white-faced and unrested. I could see that she had pushed herself as far as she could. Maureen was already burdened with problems, and this move was more than she could handle.

I took her to a doctor and, while she waited in the other room, told him the whole story from the beginning. He saw her for only a few minutes alone. When he returned, he said without hesitation, "It's anorexia nervosa."

I wasn't really shocked. I knew that there was something seriously wrong. I was even relieved that he hadn't told me that she was having some kind of nervous breakdown. My main reaction was, "OK, now we know what we are dealing with. I had hoped that she didn't have anorexia nervosa, but since she does—what do we do now?"

The doctor said that Maureen was severely underweight and had to gain weight immediately. She weighed seventy-five pounds! Though she was only five feet tall and small-boned, that was far below what a fifteen-year-old should weigh. I felt shocked and ashamed. I had known she was underweight, but I had had no idea it was that bad. Why hadn't I done something sooner?

Maureen herself seemed sobered by what we had learned. She seemed frightened by the doctor's threat that if she didn't gain a couple of pounds within the next week he would put her in the hospital and force-feed her.

When I took Maureen back to the doctor to be weighed the next week, we were all relieved to find that she had put on two pounds. The downward trend had been reversed, but now she had to struggle to get her weight up to something nearer normal. I told myself that Maureen had had enough of a shock to give her the incentive to get her weight up at last.

At least now that we knew what Maureen's problem was, we could

10

put a name to it and deal with it as other parents had. I knew it wouldn't be easy, but I thought of it as starting up a steep hill after we had been wandering around lost at the bottom. The top of that hill was in sight, and I knew that with love and guidance Maureen would make it over the top. Perhaps it is just as well that I did not know how far away the top of the hill really was and what a rocky, tortuous path lay ahead of Maureen.

* * *

We all started out very bravely. We moved into our new house and Maureen settled into her new school. But she missed her friends in Kamloops and the feeling of being someone special that she had enjoyed the previous year. She continued to study long and hard, but no teacher took her aside and told her she was wonderful and different. She ate her meals, though they were still quite small, and tried to supplement them with milkshakes. She assured Dale and me once again that she was really trying to gain weight. While she did seem to be making an honest attempt, the scale wouldn't go over eighty pounds.

After a few weeks, the doctor told us that Maureen couldn't seem to do any better on her own and that he wanted her so see the local pediatrician, Dr. Tom Morrow. Dr. Morrow had had some experience with anorexia nervosa and was willing to try to help Maureen.

After examining her and talking to her for a while, he came back to talk to me. He said that the main thing he was concerned about was her depression. I knew that she had been in low spirits over the past year, but it troubled me to hear the doctor use the label "depression." I thought it only natural that she should feel sad because of her poor health and lack of energy. I knew that she got very upset when she found fallen strands of her hair. But somehow, to me, the word "depression" made things seem even more serious. Again I felt the weight of guilt. It was bad enough to have my child diagnosed as anorexic, and now she had been diagnosed as depressed too. The word called to mind images of people driven to hopelessness by an unbearable life. I struggled to maintain my conviction that I had not done anything to make her life unbearable.

Then Dr. Morrow told me that he had asked Maureen if she had ever thought of suicide. She said she had but had dismissed the

11

idea as selfish. She promised him she would not take her life.

Suicide! Here was something I hadn't thought of. While I was sure that Maureen meant to keep her promise, I felt further burdened by the thought that she had even entertained such an idea. Although I felt that I had about all I could carry emotionally, I still didn't stumble under the load. Even the new worry labeled "suicide" didn't bring me down. I merely shifted it out of sight and carried it along with the others. Perhaps it was just that I couldn't bear to look at it at all, or perhaps I knew that Maureen had not really reached that extremity. I knew Dr. Morrow was right to bring up the subject of suicide with Maureen, and, even though it made my load even heavier, I was glad we had examined the possibility.

Over the next year, under Dr. Morrow's care, Maureen managed to gain eight pounds. But as she forced herself to eat more, it seemed that her depression deepened.

Each day she would come home from school exhausted, dragging her feet. Often the tears would roll down her cheeks, and I would take her on my knee as if she were a tiny child—and in fact she was no bigger than a ten-year-old. I would rock her and talk to her, trying to make her laugh. I knew her sense of humor and often could find something that would at least make her smile. If she could smile, exchange a few hugs with me, and have a cup of tea and one of the small snacks she allowed herself, she was usually ready to closet herself in her room again, immersed in homework.

Sometimes I would have to resort to more extreme measures. "I'll dance you!" I'd threaten. Then I'd clutch her to my bosom and cavort around the floor, singing loudly and dragging her with me. It didn't take much of this ridiculous jig to make Maureen smile.

Later she would steal out of her room for a few minutes and slide her thin arms around my neck as I was making supper. "Thank you, Mom," she'd whisper. "I don't know what I'd do without you."

In some ways I was feeling optimistic. Maureen was gaining weight, however slowly. She thought that Dr. Morrow could help her, and I thought that she was on that steep climb to recovery.

But it was around this time that I really began to suffer. For me, this period of Maureen's illness was the worst. I went to the library and began to research the causes of anorexia nervosa.

There wasn't a great deal of information available, and what there was seemed vague, contradictory, or frightening. I had a great need to know why this had happened. Why had a happy, well-loved girl fallen prey to what I couldn't deny was a mental illness? We must have done something wrong, failed her in some significant way. And the literature supported this contention. The general opinion was that girls become anorexic because of their parents — especially their mothers.

Mothers of anorexic girls are described as too demanding. They are too rigid. Their expectations for their girls are too high. The girls can't live up to these impossible standards, so they rebel by refusing to eat.

Another theory is that the mothers are weak and accommodating, with no lives of their own. Their daughters are disgusted with them and determined not to be like them. They see their mothers as passive, and they decide that rather than emulate their mothers they will control their own lives. The one thing they can control is what they eat.

I lay awake many nights as I struggled with these theories. I had always thought I had reasonable expectations for my girls. As a former teacher, I knew that children usually reach the level you expect them to reach. I expected my girls to be imaginative, creative, sensitive, and intelligent. And so they proved to be. But, I insisted to myself, I had not expected them to be the very best at everything, to compete with others, to prove themselves. If Maureen was driven, if she had impossibly high standards, she had made that choice herself. I had given her praise and reassurance, but she was often disappointed in herself.

"No," spoke the accusatory voice in my mind, "you must have been mistaken. You must have somehow communicated the message that you weren't satisfied with her the way she was, that you demanded more of her."

I wondered if I were weak and accommodating, like the mothers described in one of the books. I had always thought I was easy-going, flexible, and adaptable. Could it be that Maureen saw these characteristics as weakness? My nasty inner voice told me that Maureen was sick because I had never had the guts to stand up for my rights.

Then I read that anorexic girls were the daughters of women who had been educated for careers but had given them up to raise their families. Somehow they were taking their frustrations out on their poor families.

13

Well, it was true that I had stopped my part-time teaching job when Maureen was three and had never gone back. "But I don't want to teach. I'd rather stay home. I wasn't even a very good teacher!" I protested to myself.

Back came the accusatory voice. "You just think you'd rather stay at home. Really you are frustrated and miserable and you've taken it out on your child."

But I was most shaken by a book called *Psychosomatic Families: Anorexia Nervosa in Context* by Salvador Minuchin, Bernice L. Rosman, and Lester Baker. The authors claim that an anorexic child is like a red light identifying a sick family. To my horror, I recognized many of the characteristics of my own beloved family in the pages of this book.

We are a family that does things together, and we show a lot of affection toward each other. The authors of this book say that the families of anorexics exhibit "excessive togetherness and sharing" and a great deal of concern for each other's welfare. They also say that loyalty and protection take precedence over autonomy and self-realization and that family loyalty and denial of self for another's benefit are highly valued.

That certainly sounded like my family. We tried to think of others first. That is a basic part of our Christian beliefs. Oh, but that was mentioned too: "Usually a strong religious or ethical code is used as a rationale for avoiding conflict."

The book calls these families "enmeshed," meaning that they are too concerned with each other and caught in their pattern of family life. Children in enmeshed families are conditioned to act as the family expects and feel great responsibility for not embarrassing the family in front of other people. Consensus is extremely important to the enmeshed family, and usually one of the parents places a high value on avoiding conflict. The authors call the happiness of such families "pseudoharmony." In other words, no matter how much the family of an anorexic may claim to be a happy family, these therapists are convinced that such families are only trying to cover over their conflict and trouble; they are not in any true sense "happy."

I began to look at my family through different eyes. Night after night I lay awake analyzing my relationships with my children, my husband, and even my God.

Our deeply held religious beliefs are at the very heart of our family. We believe that the father is the divinely appointed head of the family. This is not an excuse for dictatorship, for the husband must love his wife as his own flesh—a huge responsibility. But now I began to wonder if I had been storing up resentment for this arrangement, even though I wasn't aware of it.

I had long ago accepted the fact that my husband is a workaholic. He's an achiever, a doer. He has difficulty stopping and smelling the roses. In fact, I am sure that many times he has been unaware that there were roses to smell. In contrast, I have been known to smell the roses at great length, often when I should have been washing the kitchen floor or doing some other chore.

Dale also suffers from a painful disease of the spine that often makes him impatient and irritable. I thought I had managed well over the years. Usually I ignored his critical remarks—sometimes grimly, but usually with a sense of humor. I was also convinced that, as the proverb says, "a soft answer turns away wrath" and thought that I had often avoided unpleasantness by refusing to lose my temper. Did I really suffer from a "fear of conflict"? Were the Christian teachings by which I tried to live my life wrong? Had I turned Maureen into a sick child by being mild and turning the other cheek? I had thought I showed strength by refusing to respond in kind. Had it really been weakness?

Before, I had always felt lucky, even smug, that I was so happily married. Dale and I had married after a stormy but romantic court-ship. He was the only man I ever wanted to marry, and I felt secure in knowing that we had married for life. I thought he was difficult sometimes, but we had so many wonderful times together that I always felt the good outweighed the bad. Our love for each other, for our children, and for our God was the very foundation of our lives. Our interests centered around this love. We had always said that a happy family life was the most important thing to us. Why should I feel guilty about that now?

But I started responding to Dale differently. If he was tired and irritable, I no longer felt sorry for him. Instead, I began to feel sorry for myself. Why should I have to put up with his irritability?

Now when he came home from work unexpectedly, looked around in disgust, and remarked, "This place looks like a pigpen," I didn't just shrug and think that he must have a problem at work. Now I was much more likely to retaliate. "It doesn't always look like

15

a pigpen!" I'd say. "The house is a little untidy at this particular moment. Why do you have to exaggerate and make things sound so bad?"

I soon found that my attitude only made things worse. To add to our pain of having a sick child, we were not getting along very well. I was watching Dale for every little sign that he was "dictatorial," and I was determined that I would no longer be "passive."

I had always shared my problems with Dale, but now the blame I was attaching to him made it impossible for me to go to him with my worries. When I told him about the theory that sick families cause anorexia nervosa, he dismissed the idea immediately. "That's nonsense," he said. So I continued to carry my guilty burden alone.

As I tried to cope with the idea that our relationship had made our daughter sick, the guilt I felt made my life almost unbearable. Before I started learning about anorexia, I had been able to keep my eyes on a bright future when Maureen would be healthy, happy, and normal. I told myself that things were bad at present but that they would surely start to improve if I could just keep going. Now, for the first time, I felt my feet slipping from under me. I wondered how I would be able to carry on.

Dale and I celebrated our twentieth wedding anniversary at this time, and my heart was heavy as I put on the bright pink dress that he loved. We had always regarded our anniversary as a special day in our lives, and twenty years was an especially important anniversary. We were both quiet as we drove to our favorite restaurant. As we sat over a glass of wine, we reminisced about some of our other anniversaries. ● ● ●

"Remember the year I was pregnant with DaleAnn and we drove to Kelowna for dinner? I had fresh strawberries and cream for dessert. And I wore the blue maternity dress that I had made. We were so proud of that big tummy of mine!"

"The year you were pregnant with Maureen you wore the same dress," Dale said. "She was born only four days after our anniversary. I bought you a rose corsage, and a stranger came up and whispered in your ear that you looked beautiful. And you did!"

I reminded him of another anniversary. "Things weren't always that great, were they? Remember the year you were building our first house? You labored night and day, but I thought you'd at least take time to celebrate our anniversary. I made a special supper and a fancy cake. You ate the supper all right, but before I had finished cutting the cake, you were gone, hammer in your hand! But we just laughed about it later. I was proud to have a husband who worked so hard for his family."

As we recalled some of our shared past, I glanced at the beautiful pearl ring Dale had given me that year as an anniversary gift. He could be so thoughtful and sensitive. Looking at him across the table, tears in my eyes, I realized how important he was to me.

"I've been a fool!" I thought. "I love my husband very much. I don't want to lose him. I want to continue the happy marriage we've enjoyed for twenty years. We've worked long and hard to find the balance we need to be happy and I've been upsetting the balance just because of other people's theories. How can it benefit Maureen if her parents are quarreling constantly? Or if they end up in a divorce?" Whatever the "experts" had to say, I decided I was going to work to maintain my happy marriage.

So I stopped answering back every time Dale said something critical, and I tried harder to appreciate him for his good qualities. Within a few days our old relationship was restored as we fell back into our old pattern. I felt much better about myself and about my marriage as tension between us relaxed. I stopped feeling so sorry for myself and realized that Dale deserved some sympathy too. After all, he was Maureen's father, and he was worried about her too. He said he was afraid to hug her because she felt so fragile. His instinct told him to force her to eat; yet his common sense told him that was not the answer. He knew she had to decide to eat enough on her own, but it was extremely frustrating for him to watch his skinny child picking listlessly at her food.

I would see him watching her, his face tense. I would hold my breath, praying silently that he wouldn't launch into a lecture. After the meal, when Maureen had gone to her room, he would slam his fist into his hand. "It's so hard for me not to insist that she eat more! I would just love to grab her and shake her!"

Somehow I managed to convince Dale that forcing Maureen to give up control over what she ate was not the answer to the problem. But even as I spoke to him calmly and logically, my heart was crying out, "We have a sick child. Sick children come from sick families. Therefore, we are a sick family."

I hoped I would find some expert who would prove me wrong in

17

my conclusion. I took my notes and went to talk to Dr. Morrow. He assured me that Maureen probably would have developed this problem even if—as he put it—she had been adopted at birth by a troop of circus performers. He thought her problem lay in her basic personality. He said that she was a perfectionist; that she regarded fat as unacceptable, even contemptible; that she was very competitive; and that she thought that being thin made her better than her peers—she had a desire to be different from other people. He also said she needed to gain more independence from Dale and me and to develop a better social life with young people her own age. She had not been socializing with anyone for quite a while—she was always studying, and she was afraid of finding herself in a situation she couldn't control where she would have to eat.

I agreed with what Dr. Morrow said. I thought that her personality had contributed to her problem. I also thought that she needed to enjoy more time with people her own age. And while it made me feel somewhat better to hear him dismiss the role of parents in causing anorexia nervosa, I still felt a certain amount of guilt. I had an image of myself as a "conciliating go-between" married to a "dictatorial" man. We were an "enmeshed family." I wanted to believe what Dr. Morrow told me, but part of me said, "He's just a small-town pediatrician. The real experts in anorexia nervosa know a lot more about it than he does."

Maureen's weight was up to eighty-eight pounds. While that wasn't a dramatic increase,I was comforted to know that the trend was up rather than down. I thought that Maureen was on the road to recovery. I tried to stay optimistic, reminding myself that she had a serious illness and that we couldn't expect her to get better overnight.

When the opportunity arose for Maureen to stay with her aunt in Vernon for a week, we decided it was a perfect chance for her to try her wings. Her weight was reasonable, she had saved some spending money, she knew several teenagers in the area, and she was determined to eat well and enjoy herself.

She had a marvelous time. She shopped and went to the beach with her friends. She managed very well without her parents around—caught the city bus uptown, handled her money sensibly, and traveled alone on the Greyhound bus coming home. And she came home six pounds thinner. She was down to eighty-two pounds.

18

Maureen explained that she couldn't look after everything. Being grown up and responsible was challenging and fun, but she couldn't force herself to eat at the same time. We all felt disappointed and discouraged.

Dr. Morrow finally broached the subject I had hoped would never arise. He thought Maureen needed to see a psychiatrist. We agreed that she would start by seeing the local doctor rather than travel to Calgary or Vancouver for treatment. We thought that we should at least try a few sessions and see how Maureen and the psychiatrist got along. He was the only one in the area, so we had no choice.

Dale and I were worried, though. We couldn't help but wonder what kind of person this psychiatrist was. We had read horror stories about psychiatrists who relate all problems to sexual repression, and we felt that we should use at least as much care in choosing a "mind" doctor as we had in choosing our family "body" doctor, if not more. We decided that I should see the psychiatrist first by myself to find out what sort of person we would be dealing with.

I waited self-consciously in the doctor's office, flipping nervously through old issues of *Life*. I scrutinized the other patients out of the corner of my eye. Manic-depressive? Schizophrenic? Psychotic? Suicidal? Homicidal? Or just sad and tired, like me?

"I'm sitting in a psychiatrist's office," I said wonderingly to myself. "What am I doing here? I hope I'm doing the right thing."

"Mrs. Ardell?" the psychiatrist called.

I stood up and followed the doctor into his office. "A miniature man," I thought. "Not much over five feet tall, small hands and feet, small, neat features."

I wasn't too surprised to note his air of superiority. "Perhaps he is superior," I thought. "I hope so."

I settled down to answer his questions and to ask a few of my own. He made it clear that he was an extremely busy man. He also wanted to know why I had come alone for the first visit. When I explained as tactfully as I could that I wanted to see what kind of person would be poking around in my daughter's head, he sternly informed me that he too had a right to check out our family. "I may not take your daughter as a patient. If the family dynamics are too complex, I may refuse to handle the case."

When I told him that Maureen herself was reluctant to see him, he told me to explain to her that he was a surgeon as well as a psychiatrist. I guess that was supposed to encourage her somehow.

We set an appointment. Because I had read that anorexics need independence and that many of their problems are caused by over-protective mothers, I mentioned that Maureen could walk over after school. "Oh, no," the doctor said with a reproachful look. "She'll feel nervous and apprehensive the first time. You should bring her. Besides, I'll want to talk to you after I've met her."

Maureen did not go to her appointment happily, but she realized that she needed help. She was sorry that Dr. Morrow felt he had failed with her; I think she really went to the psychiatrist to please Dr. Morrow. • • •

Maureen was in the psychiatrist's office for half an hour before she came out and said that he wanted to see me. He told me smugly that he thought Maureen had responded very well to him and that he thought he could help her. But I would have to promise not to interfere—not to comment on what Maureen did or didn't eat and not to ask whether her weight was up or down. I had never hovered over her, counting bites of food, or stood over her shoulder as she weighed herself, so it didn't seem a difficult promise.

Maureen was quiet on the way home.

"He's a twit," she said at last.

I didn't comment; he was also our only hope at this point.

"He said there's too much love in our family and not enough hate."

Later she told me that he had insisted I was overprotective.

"She is not," Maureen had replied disgustedly.

"Then what is she doing out in the waiting room?" he asked triumphantly.

"You told her that you wanted to talk to her after."

"Oh."

Fall and winter passed. The guilt and pain I was carrying were eased somewhat by the fact that Maureen was in professional hands. I had been told not to comment on her food choices or her weight and I didn't, although she seemed to be eating much the same as she had been for the past couple of years. I had stuck to my decision not to let Maureen's illness ruin my relationship with my husband and had returned to my former habits of avoiding conflict with him. The warmth and support that I received from our close relationship made it easier for me to carry on. I had also made a conscious decision to maintain my faith in God. I felt that if the teachings of Christ were wrong, then we were all without hope. There is enough pain in the world without adding selfishness and lack of concern for others. So my faith was of great comfort to me at this time also. But basically what I was doing was holding my breath, just waiting to see if this doctor had any answers for us.

Maureen saw the doctor once a month. She said that she wasn't supposed to tell me what they talked about because she had to learn not to be so dependent. Her depression seemed much the same as it had when she was going to Dr. Morrow. Only now when she was depressed and I reached out to hug her, I would stop in confusion, thinking that perhaps I was prolonging her illness, making her more dependent on me, keeping her a child. Other times I would mentally stick out my tongue at the "experts" and hug her anyway.

To my relief, I found a sane and sensible book — *Anorexia Nervosa: A Guide for Sufferers and Their Families* — by R.L. Palmer, who downplays the responsibility of parents for the illness. He suggests that societal attitudes toward women and contemporary ideas of what a young woman should look like, as reflected in advertising, for example, play a part in the development of anorexia nervosa. He mentions the theories about families that insist they are happy yet force their daughters to be overcompliant and, eventually, rebellious, but he points out that many families of anorexic girls are "overtly hostile, disturbed, ill or absent," and that such a family is "characterized by its chaos rather than its rigid expectations." Dr. Palmer seems to lean toward the "fear of growing up" theory, but he states that a wide range of influences are probably at work.

I found great refreshment in this sympathy for parents. He recognizes that it is difficult for parents to watch their child waste away when it seems that all she has to do in order to correct the problem is eat. And I felt better about the length of time it took me to acknowledge Maureen's illness when I read: "To acknowledge to oneself that one's daughter has anorexia nervosa may carry the flavour of failure as a parent. . . . It is natural to postpone the painful acknowledgment of trouble until reality forces a readjustment. Paradoxically it may seem to the parent that even to think in terms of a problem may increase the chances of it occurring and the temptation to close the eyes and hope is very real." He says further that "Parents may feel wary of putting themselves into the hands of a doctor who might turn out to be critical and scornful of an illness which can be so easily construed as in some way the fault of the subject or her family."

I found Dr. Palmer's book to be realistic but hopeful. He warns that one should look for personal growth and development in an anorexic rather than a cure, and I felt sure that his closing prediction would prove to be true: "The road to recovery can be long and tedious.... There will characteristically be disappointments. It is best to travel hopefully, but to expect a long journey."

Another book I found reassuring was *The Psychological Society* by Martin L. Gross, who claims that our society is too prone to see things psychologically. Although he never mentions anorexia nervosa, he says that, in general, we are far too eager to blame parents for problems young people have. Speaking of parents, he says: "Too often they view themselves as the cause of the problem and therefore the source of the cure. Aided by unsubtle propaganda of the Psychological Society, parents come away convinced that they have committed the *modern crime of inexpert parenthood*, one of the most heinous sins of our era."

Mr. Gross asks the same question I asked myself: "What did parents do wrong? Nothing in particular, everything in general. They assumed too much, tried too much, hoped too much. The seeds of their frustration were there all the time: in their relative impotence; in the general untruthfulness of psychological theorems and platitudes; in their false anxieties; and in the overwhelming power of biology and the idiosyncrasies of the human animal."

I had certainly been eager to accept all the blame for Maureen's illness. Now I began to see that at least some of the blame belonged on Maureen herself. Despite her protestations to the contrary, she still did not seem ready to give up her unreasonable behavior. She frowned and sulked and sighed if I happened to have a meal ready a few minutes early. The amount of food she served herself looked pathetically small to Dale and me. The only dessert she would eat was a small serving of vanilla ice cream. Sometimes I saw her measuring out one teaspoonful of margarine for her bread.

During the winter Maureen began to refer to herself as a "recovering anorexic," but she still looked pretty much the same to me — pale, thin, and listless. Her hair had become quite thin as well.

Like most anorexics, she suffered from the cold. She didn't have enough fat cells to keep herself warm, so she was always bundled up in layers of clothing — a shirt, a sweater, and then a blazer. It was obvious that she was very skinny, but I kept my promise not to pry and trusted that her doctor was handling her problems.

Then one day in early spring, the psychiatrist phoned Dale at work. He had just discovered that Maureen was down to sixty-two pounds. He said that she had been losing weight steadily all winter but that he had thought he would be able to help her get it under control. But now he was frightened. He had never mentioned it before, but she had lost twenty pounds under his care.

Dale and I were sick with disappointment and fear. The doctor phoned the next morning to say that he had worried about Maureen all night. If she caught flu or even a bad cold, she could die. He wanted her in the hospital immediately. I picked her up at school and took her straight to the Cranbrook hospital. Before she had time to realize what was happening, she was in bed.

Anorexics are typically agreeable and cooperative. Once again, Maureen displayed these characteristics. Yes, she realized that she had to gain weight immediately. Yes, she could see that she was emaciated and that her condition was dangerous. Yes, she would talk to the dietitian and try to eat more.

"Mom, I don't understand how I got so low. Maybe there is something else wrong with me. I've been eating pretty well. I count my calories, and I get about two thousand calories every day."

Looking at her, I knew that no normal person could eat that much and be that thin. She almost had me convinced that there was some physical cause for her thinness until I had a talk with the dietitian. She had been keeping track of everything Maureen ate for a few days, and it appeared that Maureen was badly over-estimating her calorie consumption. She was actually only getting one thousand calories a day, or even less. Maureen seemed genuinely surprised to discover the low calorie count of some of her favorite foods.

She nibbled and snacked and complained of being uncomfortably full, but she did get her weight up a couple of pounds. In the meantime her doctor had been in touch with Dr. Lester Sandor in Vancouver, who was reported to have amazing success treating anorexics. We were all hoping that Maureen could see him soon.

This hospitalization in Cranbrook was obviously a temporary measure, and no one seemed sure what to do with her. ● ●

One day one of the nurses at the hospital took Maureen into her office for a little chat. There she propounded her theory that Maureen was "refusing to accept her sexuality" and insisted that she read a pamphlet on masturbation. A few days later, the psychiatrist came up with another theory: Maureen's religious upbringing had given her a terrible guilt complex.

By this time, Maureen, Dale, and I were all tired of people's guessing and theorizing. We longed to meet someone who knew what he or she was talking about, and we looked forward to Maureen's hospitalization in Vancouver with something like relief. Perhaps someone would finally help us.

● ● ● But just as Maureen was about to be released from the Cranbrook hospital, we got the news that the psychiatric ward at Shaughnessy Hospital, where Dr. Sandor practices, had been completely flooded by a broken water main and Dr. Sandor did not know when he could take Maureen. So we had to take her home, armed with calorie-counting books and a tiny kitchen scale. The staff at the Cranbrook hospital had been carefully counting Maureen's calorie intake and we were to keep it up at home.

What agony that turned out to be! Maureen never took her eyes off me as I prepared her meals. We rigidly followed the hospital outline—she wouldn't let me deviate in the slightest. "That's not a medium orange, that's a large," she would say. "I won't eat it."

For the first time, I could see the anorexic toughness under her sweetness. It was difficult to deal reasonably with the unreasonable determination of a true abstainer.

Maureen had to see the number on the scale as I weighed out her cheese slices. If it was even the barest fraction over the prescribed weight, she would shave off the sides of the cheese until it satisfied her. Now that she was home, the house was filled with tension, which often broke into warfare at mealtime. Maureen glared at us with hatred as we adhered to the hospital outline of meals. She did eat as much as the dietitian instructed her to—but not one mouthful more.

All the conflict in our house centered around food. Maureen said she wanted to gain weight, but she hated for me to have any voice in what she ate or how much. Now that the hospital had provided a list of foods and the amount that she should eat, she could no

24

longer nibble at things and pretend that she was diligently striving to gain weight. I was unhappy because I was forced to see that Maureen had been lying to me, and probably to herself, about her desire to gain weight. Dale was angry because the problem had been dragging on for so long and Maureen was not any better. He was angry that she should behave so unreasonably over something like one extra tablespoon of cottage cheese. Maureen was tense and angry too. She could no longer pretend that she wanted to gain weight or that she was recovering from her illness. She had liked it better when her father and I had no part in assigning her portions of food and when we thought she was really trying to put on weight.

I felt that we were doing nothing to help Maureen get better but were just keeping her alive until she could get to Dr. Sandor. As for the causes of Maureen's illness, I didn't even care anymore. Looking around our grim dinner table, I couldn't help but think that if she had gotten sick because of a happy family, she was a lot sicker in one that was now miserable.

We finally received the welcome news that Maureen could be admitted to Shaughnessy Hospital the following week. After our experiences with the psychiatrist in Cranbrook, we were nervous about meeting Dr. Sandor. What kind of person would he be? What approach would he take? Would he attack us or our religious beliefs?

We went to meet him before we took Maureen to the ward. He was a short, fair man of indeterminate age, relaxed and amiable. As he discussed the background of anorexia nervosa, we tried to concentrate on his words and appear fairly intelligent. But his casual manner, his obvious erudition, and his confidence that he could help Maureen reassured us tremendously, and we began to feel a little optimistic.

Maureen was admitted to the hospital, and we all walked over to the temporary psychiatric ward. Maureen, Dale, and I smiled brightly at each other and repeated endless assurances that now all would be well. Finally we had found someone who seemed to know how to treat anorexia nervosa.

Still, Maureen was apprehensive. Would she be held down and fed intravenously? Would she be forced to eat the foods she had come to abhor?

And I was still afraid that someone would sit us down and tell us what bad parents Dale and I were and how our sick personalities had caused Maureen's illness. Or insist that Maureen was sexually repressed by our religious beliefs and that free sexual expression was the only hope of cure. Dale and I were prepared to grab her and run if anyone attacked our family or our faith.

When we left, Dr. Sandor followed us down the hall and said that he would like to ask us something personal.

"Does your religion teach..." he began. I felt Dale stiffen beside me.

"...that it is right to emphasize the outward person rather than the inner, spiritual qualities?"

"No. Of course not," I replied warily.

"Have you ever told Maureen that?"

"I haven't emphasized it lately."

"Why not?"

"Because she feels bad enough. I don't want her to feel any more guilty."

"Well, she *should* feel guilty! Tell her that God doesn't want her to abuse her body for such a worldly, selfish purpose — for mere vanity."

Relief washed over me. What a refreshing attitude! Dr. Sandor obviously intended to use Maureen's religious beliefs to work for her, not against her. We left the hospital feeling much better than we had for a long time.

It appeared that Maureen would need to be in the hospital for at least three months, and I needed to be near at hand. We were fortunate to find a place for me to board only a few blocks from the hospital.

After we took my suitcase to my room, Dale and I kissed goodbye with brave smiles. He had to fly home to Cranbrook to get back to work. After he had left, I went to Shaughnessy to see how Maureen was.

We visited for a while, but she was feeling a little glum and cried when I left — although she tried to hide it. I was feeling low myself as I left the hospital to catch my bus.

I stood numbly at the bus stop, rain dripping down my neck. A young man galloped across the street from Children's Hospital, which is next door to Shaughnessy, and stood waiting nearby. I carefully avoided his eyes, struggling with the depression that was pressing down on me.

"I guess you're used to waiting for the bus, eh?" the young man asked." "You city people do it all the time."

I had to smile. "I'm visiting here from a pretty small town." (I even considered saying, "I'm a stranger here myself.")

"Oh, really? You're just visiting here too, are you? My wife might lose our baby, so they flew her here this morning and a specialist is with her now."

He really just needed someone to talk to about his problems, and my heart went out to him as he tried to put up a brave front. I willingly listened to the story of how he and his wife had tried for some time to have a baby, their joy when his wife conceived, and their horror when things began to go wrong. I sympathized and encouraged him with the usual platitudes. Finally he asked if I had been visiting someone at the hospital.

"Yes, my sixteen-year-old daughter," I told him. I thought of his baby struggling for life and how easy and healthy my pregnancy with Maureen had been, what a beautiful, strong baby she had been, and how unthinkingly optimistic I had been about her future. Sadness rose up in me and I answered him in a way I would not ordinarily have talked to a stranger.

"She has anorexia nervosa. She weighs under seventy pounds and has to battle for every ounce she gains. She's depressed, and I don't know what to say to her anymore. What can you say to someone who is terrified of something as basic as food?"

It made him uncomfortable, of course. He didn't know what to say. He was suddenly cast out of his self-absorption into a view of someone else's tragedy. And with a difference. I sensed that if I had said, "She has cancer," he would have expressed real sorrow and we could have shared a common struggle against nature, which sometimes unaccountably goes awry. But, underneath my matter-of-fact statement, I could hear my unspoken words, "What did I do to her?" And the young man's eyes were saying to me, "What did you do to her?" He was intelligent, modern, educated — a teacher, he told me. He knew as well as I did that children who were on the psych ward had been failed in some fundamental way by their parents.

As I lay in my strange, new bed that night, I reflected on all that had brought me to this time and place. I had felt hopeful before — was I doomed to disappointment again? Or did Dr. Sandor really know what he was doing? What was Maureen thinking in her dismal hospital room at that minute? And what did the next three months hold for her?

DAUGHTER

I thought I would feel really scared when we got to Vancouver and walked through the hospital where I would be staying. But all I felt was the same old nothingness I had felt for three years. I was playing a part, trying to react as a sixteen-year-old girl should. But there was just nothing there. Occasionally, I would have the sensation that I was a character in my own dream. I felt that this couldn't really be happening.

The psychiatrist in Cranbrook said that I was both wise and brave to decide at last that I couldn't get rid of this sickness by myself. He said that I needed help if I didn't want to die. "I wish you could think of this as a positive experience," he said. I wished I could too.

I had been anorexic for three years before being admitted to Shaughnessy Hospital. I was five feet tall, and in those three years I had gone from 105 to 62 pounds. Sometimes I could see what all the fuss was about—I could understand the dangers of continuing to live the way I was. But most of the time I just didn't want to eat. I didn't feel normal; I always knew I was different. But at the same time I felt as if I were doing a reasonable and good thing. Somehow I felt that the less I ate, the purer I became. I felt cleaner inside.

Looking back, I can see that the problem started when I entered grade nine. I guess I have always felt in some way threatened by my sister, DaleAnn. She was so bright and popular. When I went into grade nine, she left junior high and started grade eleven in a new school. I decided then that I would make my mark. I guess you could say I did.

Shortly after school began, I started to really hate myself. I wanted to change everything about me. I wanted to lose a few pounds, reshape my body, and improve my marks. And I did. I developed a self-control that shocked everyone, even me. I never stopped eating completely, but when I was fourteen I started to cut down. I ate as little as Mom and Dad would allow.

Then came the laws. I began to put myself under strict food rules. One of these was that any fats, like butter or margarine or oil, were evil. I could not eat them. If Mom forgot that I didn't eat these things and buttered my toast or something, I could not eat it. Later I would allow myself half a teaspoon of carefully measured margarine a day. I liked to have a certain spoon, fork, and knife, and I didn't really feel comfortable eating with different ones. I also thought that the later I ate a meal, the better I was. To me, a late meal meant I had suffered longer and so deserved to eat. If I ever ate what I thought was too much, or broke one of my food rules, I had to starve myself even more for the next few days.

I learned the calorie content of every food I might be confronted with. Several times I got caught reading calorie books during class. I had a remarkable memory for these figures. A cup of skim milk has eighty-nine calories. A large carrot has forty. Beef is more fattening than pork. I never forgot this information.

At the same time that I was rigidly controlling my calorie intake, I was obsessed with food. I used to hang around the bakery department of the grocery stores. I liked to see the food and smell it and yet know that I could resist, that I was strong enough never to eat that kind of food again. I also cut pictures of food out of magazines. Just seeing it was enough for me—I didn't have to eat it. I decorated my room with these pictures because food was really the most important thing in my life.

Soon the pounds began to fall off. They came off slowly at first and I felt proud of myself. But then they came off quickly. My new-found self-control quickly spread to other aspects of my life. I threw myself into my schoolwork with ridiculous vigor. I had assignments ready weeks in advance, and my marks went from B's to straight A's. On weekends, my schoolwork came before recreation or pleasure. And my work was never done; I could always find more to do. At Christmas time when I was in grade nine, I studied for midterm exams until I was sick. I was eating next to nothing and working myself to the limit. I was so thin, pale, and tired that people asked me if I were anemic. My parents insisted that I stay home for a few days and go to bed. But I was always getting up to study. If they insisted that I do something else, I would set my alarm for 5:00 A.M.

29

and study by flashlight. Around this time Mom tried making me drink milkshakes so that I would put on some weight. I flushed them all down the toilet.

My weight soon dropped to eighty-five, and then Mom and Dad really started to worry. At first they had been delighted with my self-discipline and good marks, but now they began to think something was wrong.

In the meantime, I was beginning to withdraw. I worked harder than ever at school and started practicing the piano more than I ever had before. I was a little worried because I was losing so much weight, but it felt good to have what I thought was absolute control over my body and mind. But I also became plagued with guilt—I felt guilty about everything I did. It was then that I first started to notice a change in my moods. I couldn't understand why the little things that used to be so enjoyable now brought me little or no pleasure. I would rather stay at home and study than go out with friends and do things I used to love. My teachers and the other kids at school admired me, and I was proud of myself too. But I worried about things constantly and easily became irritable. I was always so tired that I couldn't do anything but sit in my room and study.

When we moved to Cranbrook, my weight suddenly dropped to seventy-five pounds. People began to comment on my appearance. Once DaleAnn saw me without my clothes on and screamed that I looked like a starvation victim from a refugee camp. At the time, I thought she was jealous. Mom felt terribly guilty, as if my condition were somehow her fault. People asked her why I was so skinny and pale. They wondered why my hair was so dull and I looked so sick. Everyone offered suggestions, remedies, medicines, and doctors. One person said, "Let her come home with me for a few days. I'll fix her up." I just wished they would all mind their own business.

When my aunt came for a visit, she had a fit. She turned angrily on my mother. "That girl is going to starve herself to death!" she screamed. "Are you just going to stand there and watch her do it?" Mom cried after she left. She just didn't know what to do. Mom and Dad didn't want to physically force me to eat for fear of making the problem worse. I think if they had ever done that I would have been forced to start vomiting.

I kept getting worse. I made my own lunch for school and watched everything Mom made for supper. I always had to supervise and make sure that she didn't slip in something I was unaware of or hadn't included in my daily calorie allowance. I developed more food laws. I never consciously made these up; they were suddenly just there. And I was more restricted than I had been before. For example, I could not eat pancakes. I used to love them, and it was this fondness that now made them forbidden. Enjoyment to me was close to immorality. A really crazy rule was my ice cream law. If ice cream was on my schedule for the day and I ate it before supper, then it had to be in a cone; if I ate it for dessert, it had to be in a dish.

The truth was that I was afraid to eat. I was scared to gain weight because I didn't know what I would turn into.

One day Mom took me downtown and told me to pick out all the foods I loved. She said she would make my favorite dishes if I wanted. She must have been really worried. I felt like a spoiled brat, and that made me feel guilty and upset about what I was doing. So I tried to eat more food, or at least foods with a higher calorie content. But while our grocery bill went up, my weight kept going down. I just couldn't do it. When I think of all the snacks that I hid under my bed, I feel sick. I couldn't eat them, but neither could I let Mom down by telling her that I refused to. I was still not ready to accept the fact that I was anorexic and needed help.

My family began to watch what I ate very closely. I had to start using different tactics to get out of eating. I never induced vomiting, but I used other anorexic ploys. For example, if I didn't want to eat something, I'd wait until no one was watching and then slip it into my napkin so that I could dispose of it later. I would say that I hated certain foods, like whipped cream, and that I just couldn't eat them. I could even make myself believe I hated them.

I used to complain that I was too full to put another bite in my mouth. Mom began to insist on making my lunch for school. The huge lunches she gave me just made me angry. I resented being told what to eat. I would take my sandwich and scrape all the butter off the bread and then take out half the filling. This ritual had to be performed in secret or I would be in trouble, so I often had to do it in my bedroom before school, or even in the bathroom. This practice seemed disgusting, even to me, but I felt I had no choice. And every morning as my sister and I ran down the dirt path to catch our school bus, I would drop bits of that morning's toast as inconspicuously as I could. At times I yearned to be able to eat normally, but when I tried I felt too guilty to continue.

When my weight kept dropping, I became concerned and made great resolutions to eat. But when I tried putting them into action at mealtimes, I just couldn't do it. I was being pulled two ways. I felt terrible if I didn't eat, but I felt weak and self-indulgent if I did. I felt very depressed.

Just as I had feared, I got caught at some of my tricks. Twice Mom found little caches of food that I had hidden. She blamed herself, and then I felt even more guilty. But the worst part was that I couldn't tell anyone my problems. True, I did have a close relationship with my mother, but I couldn't tell her what I was doing for fear that she would make me stop my behavior and eat more.

Then the real nightmare began. I had very long, thick blond hair. I had always thought that it was my greatest asset, and people often commented on it. Now it was beginning to fall out. It was barely noticeable at first, but later the strands came out in large handfuls when I ran my fingers through my hair. This upset me very much, but I still could not force myself to eat more. I told myself that I would rather be completely bald than eat what I felt was bad. The hair loss became worse and worse. There were hairs in my clothes, my plants, my food, my books, my purse, and my bed. Once our vacuum cleaner got clogged up with long blond hairs. Everywhere I looked I saw more hair, and, to me, that was just more proof that I was ugly and useless. My lost hair became an obsession. I counted hairs the way I counted calories. I used to save each one I found and put it on my bookshelf. At the end of the week, I'd put all the hairs in a box. There were hundreds of them.

During the summer, there were mornings when I felt I just couldn't get out of bed. My future seemed bleak, and my conscience bothered me about everything. I was barely fifteen, but I felt like a tired old woman. I felt ready to die.

Before going to Shaughnessy, I saw two general practitioners, one pediatrician, and one psychiatrist. I was also hospitalized once in Cranbrook. Nothing helped much. My family came to Dr. Sandor in desperation. I weighed sixty-four pounds, and according to one doctor I was consuming about eight hundred calories a day. I cried constantly. Here is the story of my struggle to gain weight and return to some semblance of normalcy.

MONDAY, MARCH 14 "Look at that girl," someone whispered. The doctor took me into a dark little room, and I stepped on the scale — sixty-four pounds. "About the size of a large turkey," he said.

So here I am. After months of apprehension, I am finally coming face to face with reality. My treatment has begun, and I hope I will come out a very different person. Not my life, but my mind is in the hands of these people. I hope I can trust them.

I'm in Shaughnessy Hospital, Vancouver, one of the best treatment centers in Canada for anorexia nervosa. I am on block A-3, but they call it C-1, the psych ward. The original C-1, where I'm supposed to be, was flooded when a water pipe there broke. The whole ward was forced to relocate. Now C-1 has to share a ward with rehabilitation. The nurse said the old facilities were much nicer, and, I must say, it wouldn't be hard to improve on this.

The ward is like a prison. The faded yellow walls are chipped and peeling. The floors are cold tile in big red and gray squares. My room, which is right across the hall from the rehabilitation ward, has three beds, but there's only me and an old lady named Clover. I have a bed with a thin yellow bedspread, a very old gray night stand with a drawer on top and a cupboard underneath (the rusted drawer makes a horrifying screech every time it is opened), a metal locker in which to hang my clothes, a small movable table, and a chair for visitors. This is my home now.

My window looks out onto another dingy gray wing of the hospital. I can see people in greens and masks, intently working on something. It makes me feel slightly sick to my stomach to think about what is going on. Like the rest of the hospital, this wing has chipped pea-green windowsills all lined up in neat rows. Some rooms are lighted; others are dark. I wonder who is behind the dark glass and what kind of pain they're feeling.

It's starting to get dark now. I just ran my fingers through my hair and was left with an handful of long blond strands.

I didn't expect to be admitted today. Mom and Dad and I were at Lazlos', where Mom will be living, paying the rent. While we were there, Dad phoned the hospital and was told to bring me in. The Lazlos are very nice, but I'm sure they don't understand what's wrong with me.

We were ages in admitting. There were tons of questions. Finally a volunteer brought me up to the ward. The people here scare me a little bit. Some of them are obvious psych ward material; one girl does everything in slow motion. Others look perfectly normal. It's hard to tell the nurses from the patients because everyone wears street clothes. I was afraid my shrink would make me wear pajamas and stay in bed until I put some weight on. That's what they did to me in the Cranbrook hospital. But he's allowing me to wear my clothes and walk around the ward.

After I was brought to my room, one of Dr. Sandor's nurses came in to talk to us. She was wearing cords and an angora sweater and had keys tied around her waist on a red string. Her name is Chris, and she is my primary nurse. Dr. Sandor's other nurse is Diane; I'll meet her tomorrow. Chris told us I'll be on a behavior modification program. That means I'll be rewarded with more freedom for each increase in my weight. The nurses won't monitor how much I eat, but I'll be weighed each morning and they expect to see an increase of one or two points of a kilogram each day. That comes out to two or three pounds a week!

Two days ago Dr. Sandor said that my goal weight is ninety-five pounds and that I can't leave here until that goal is reached. Thirty pounds—that sounds like so much. A long time ago I decided that if I were ever to gain weight, I would never go beyond ninety pounds. Now this person who doesn't even know me is going to force me to break my own rules. I know from experience that these laws are not broken without incredible mental anguish. I cried and even asked my parents to leave the room so that I could bargain privately with Dr. Sandor. Of course he stood his ground. Now I have calmed down and started to accept the facts. I don't want to think of ninety-five right now. That's a long way into the future. I'll take it one day at a time.

Chris said I will experience a lot of fright as my body starts to change. For example, I'm always cold right now. I have to dress in layers: long underwear, shirt, wool sweater, and jacket. My fingernails are always purple. I haven't even had to wear antiperspirant for two years, because I never sweat. But as the weight goes on, I'll have some fat cells to keep me warm. This is going to be hard to adjust to. Chris also said that absolutely no tight-fitting clothes are allowed. As anorexics gain weight, it can be terrifying to find that their clothes no longer fit. I can certainly understand that. One thing that really scares me is that visiting hours are only from four to eight. I feel lonely already.

The dietitian came in to give me a supper menu to fill out. I expected her to say, "Today you have to have spaghetti and meatballs." Instead she said, "How about a fruit salad?" I was so relieved, I just nodded. While she was still there, Dr. Sandor came in to see me. "So, you want to be a missionary," he said. "Tell me, have you ever seen a missionary without a body? Ah, 'the spirit is willing, but the flesh is weak.'" I had to laugh.

After I unpacked my things, Chris showed me around the ward. The bathroom is old and dingy. Next to it is a shower room that we can use after 9:30 A.M. if none of the rehabilitation patients want it.

At the end of the hallway, there's a sort of lounge where all the patients can get together to play games, watch TV, or talk. Chris introduced me to everyone, but they were mostly old people. There was one young girl who looks about eighteen, but she's really twenty-three. Her name is Samantha. She's short and stocky, with a round, childish face. Although she is quite attractive, she looks strained and sad.

At mealtime, everybody comes down here, gets his or her tray off the cart, and eats in the lounge. Chris said that for the time being I can eat in my room if I want. I do want to. I don't like people watching me eat. I feel as if they're catching me doing something naughty and unclean. Sometimes people just like to see what an anorexic eats. To me, eating is a very personal activity, and I feel that it is my business and no one else's. Fortunately, we have lots of choice in what we eat, and the food is very good.

There is a whole list of activities for patients, including swimming and an aerobics class. But I'm not sure if I'll be allowed to do any of them. The staff has placed me on level three of a five-level system. This means I get hourly checks and am confined to the ward except when accompanied by a nurse or responsible adult, such as my parents or a visitor over the age of nineteen. As I gain weight I'll move to level four, which allows me to walk anywhere within the hospital grounds. Later I'll be able to go to the hospital cafeteria and choose my own meals. I'll also be allowed special day or weekend passes. When I reach level five, I'll be allowed to go wherever I want during the day as long as I say where I'm going and sign in and out.

There is a big chalkboard in the hallway that lists meetings the patients must attend. Fortunately, Dr. Sandor's eating-disorder patients don't have to go, since their main objective is to gain weight. Every Monday the rest of the patients attend what's called a goals group. Here they decide what they will work on for the week. I saw a handwritten list with things on it like this: "Bill's goal is to talk to his mother on Thursday." I think my own personal goal will be to reach sixty-six pounds by next Monday.

Mom and Dad went for supper and then took me around the hospital so I could get used to it. Now I know how to get to the cafeteria, the gift shop, the library, and Children's Hospital. I also know how to get to the Jean Matheson Pavilion to attend weekly group meetings with Dr. Sandor and other anorexic girls. Of course I can't go to any of these places alone—I'll have to have an escort.

It was sad to see Dad go. I won't see him again for months! It's funny how this crisis has drawn us closer. I want to get better for him.

After they left, Samantha, the girl I met earlier, came in to see me. She is bulimic, and we both talked quite openly about our problems. She's been through a lot. Like countless other bulimics, Samantha goes on horrible binges, during which she consumes huge amounts of food. She eats anything from doughnuts to cold leftovers and then makes herself throw it all up by sticking a finger down her throat. Then she begins the process all over again.

Samantha attends college for half the day and spends the rest of her time here on C-1. She's taking broadcasting and journalism. She used to be a top figure skater, but she had to stop skating because she was bulimic. Apparently she used to be anorexic like me and then turned bulimic. This is quite common. She's been sick for about five years.

I am going to bed feeling scared but hopeful. I keep telling myself to be calm, that everything will be OK. At least I don't feel crazy. Maybe I'll be out sooner than everyone thinks.

TUESDAY, MARCH 15 Last night when I was in bed with the lights off, Chris suddenly burst in, turned on the lights, and started a lecture: "Now, the TV is on from 4:00 P.M. to 11:00 P.M. only, and there are no rentals. We don't want you sitting around all day, getting depressed. Please give me all your money—I have to lock it up. I've put in an order of chloral hydrate for you because I've been told you don't sleep well." She asked me a dozen more questions and left without turning off the light. "Welcome to hospital life," I thought.

This morning I was glad to be able to get dressed before breakfast and not have to stay in my housecoat all day, like I had to in the Cranbrook hospital. I was weighed fairly early and found that I had lost another point of a kilogram. I have been going down a bit every day, especially since we left home a week ago. It seems as if I'm eating more and weighing less every day. Things are certainly not right.

Dr. Sandor came in to see me again. He said he knows a girl who studied Japanese and later went to be a missionary in Japan. He said she couldn't decide whether to be a missionary or an anorexic but finally decided to be a missionary. He also said, "You think you have control. But being anorexic doesn't show strength. Recovering—that's what takes the strength." I think he's right.

An endocrinologist came in and asked a bunch of questions. She said I have no reflexes. This is fairly common among people with eating disorders. Because I'm in a state of starvation, my electrolytes are out of balance and the neurons in my brain don't fire properly. This causes a lack of response in some areas.

This morning I met my secondary nurse, Diane. She seems very nice. She says that schooling is available at the Children's Hospital Monday to Friday from 9:00 to 12:00 and 1:30 to 2:30. I can start on Monday if I've shown some improvement. I'm determined to do so.

One of the first things I asked Diane about was my hair. I want to know how long it will be before it stops falling out. She said it will probably continue to fall out for up to a year after I achieve a normal weight. That's not very encouraging news. What if I'm totally bald by then? So far today I've found fifty-three long blond hairs in my bed and around my area of the room. And that's not even counting the ones in my brush.

I worked very hard on my schoolwork all day. Then, at 3:30, Diane took me over to Dr. Sandor's office for group therapy. Including me, there were six girls and one woman. Besides the woman, I was the oldest one there. Tiffany is forty-two and married, with two young children. She's the skinniest, ickiest thing I've ever seen. Her hands are a network of prominent blue veins. Her neck is a little straw trying to support her head, and her trachea is almost visible from the outside. Her clothes hang on her, just the way mine hang on me. She has those same anorexic grooves around her mouth that I do. I've noticed these lines on every anorexic I've met. They are deep

37

grooves that lie in an oval shape around the mouth. Along with sunken cheeks, they make even young girls look very old. It's quite unusual for a woman Tiffany's age to have such an acute case of anorexia. It must be very hard for her to explain to her children. It must also be hard to sit here and discuss her problems with a roomful of teenagers.

All the girls are at different stages of anorexia. One girl is 5'8½" and weighs ninety-nine pounds. She says she thinks she's "on the fat side." Another girl is well on the road to recovery, and she was a real encouragment to me. She described the way she used to feel, and I could really understand it. But she's overcoming her problems, and I know I can overcome mine too. She said, for example, that her whole life used to depend on her daily weigh-in. She had a rule: if she had gained weight, she would starve herself all day. But if she had lost weight, she would starve herself then too. She also said that when she started to recover and put on a few pounds, one of her relatives said she was looking well, not so pale. Instead of feeling good, she was scared and upset. It's hard to give up the anorexic image and way of life.

WEDNESDAY, MARCH 16 The day did not start well. At 8:30 A.M. a nurse came in and took eight tubes of my blood. At first she wasn't successful. She tried both arms two or three times, but my veins kept collapsing. It was quite painful. I started feeling sick and just about passed out. I had to keep pumping my arm. I think the poor nurse felt worse than I did. She kept saying, "Oh, please don't cry, dear—please."

Finally she got all the blood she needed. It will be tested to determine my levels of potassium, calcium, hemoglobin, sugar, and many other things. It is very common for girls with eating disorders to have a dangerously low potassium level. The body has a remarkable ability to adjust to abuse by anorexia nervosa, but it can only go so far—then things just give out. Diane says she expects two-thirds of these tests to come back abnormal, just because my body weight is so low.

Dr. Sandor came in and talked to me for a long time. He truly cares about each one of his patients. One of his patients, a twenty-five-year-old anorexic named Kim, eats dinner with Dr. Sandor's family every night, just so that he can make sure she puts something into her body.

38

I'm beginning to like Dr. Sandor more. He mentions spiritual matters quite often. Today he said, "You can never be a genuinely spiritual person and still be anorexic. How many times have you been forced to lie, cheat, and deceive people because of this condition?" There's no fooling him. He also asked, "For what noble purpose?" I had to say, "For no noble purpose at all." I was ashamed. The truth sure can hurt.

Finally Mom came. I was so glad to see her. I don't know what I'd do if she weren't here to encourage me. We are very close, and she's the only person I really trust. I can remember thinking as far back as grade four that if she ever died I would die too. I identify so closely with her that sometimes I forget that we are two separate individuals. Sometimes I think of both of us as one entity because our personalities complement each other. We do fight sometimes, but it's usually over food. She gets angry when I don't eat much.

After visiting hours, Samantha came in to talk to me for a while. I feel sorry for her. Bulimia has absolutely ruined her life. It takes up all her time and leaves her feeling digusted with herself and too ashamed and depressed to show her face in public. She went out yesterday afernoon, and, sure enough, she gave in to the binge-purge temptation while she was out. She's never been able to go for more than three days without having one of these episodes. Dr. Sandor says the trick is to resist throwing up, even after a big binge. Then maybe the bulimic will feel so lousy that she will stop her self-destructive behavior. Poor Samantha feels a great deal of guilt and self-repugnance.

I told her that I was afraid I'd become bulimic while trying to overcome my anorexia. But she said she didn't think I would since I am aware of the problem. When she became bulimic, she had no idea what was going on and for two years thought she was the only person in the world with this terrifying problem. I'm so glad I never induced vomiting or got into the bulimic rut.

THURSDAY, MARCH 17 My weight still hasn't shown any increase. Shortly before nine this morning, I was asked to go to the conference room to meet with Dr. Sandor, two social workers, and the dietitian. I had no makeup on yet, and I felt very vulnerable in front of all those people. To make matters worse, Dr. Sandor called me a liar, a cheat, and a deceiver. He may have been trying to make me angry, but I was only upset. It was a very humiliating experience. I don't think Dr. Sandor understands that my attitude is good. Maybe I am deceiving myself, I don't know. But I do know that I eat enough to feel mental and physical discomfort.

FRIDAY, MARCH 18 I can't believe it—I still haven't gained any weight. This really is a shock to me. I am increasing my intake a little bit and doing absolutely no physical exercise. For example, yesterday I ate a boiled egg and a bran muffin for breakfast, a big fruit salad with cottage cheese for lunch, a red jelly bean for a snack, and half a hamburger plus vanilla ice cream for supper. Then at bedtime I had half a muffin. And still I didn't gain any weight. Diane says I'll be here till hell freezes over. If I don't start to gain soon, there won't be any school for me. Well, I'll have to double my effort. I'm not going to be defeated by my body.

This morning I went upstairs to the diabetic clinic. The endocrinologist wanted to do some tests on me. First I had to sign a consent form saying that I was a willing participant in her study. Then she inserted a catheter into my arm and withdrew a tube of blood. After fifteen minutes she withdrew another tube. After these two samples had been taken, I was given one hundred grams of glucose mixed with milk and egg. It was so gross and disgustingly sweet that I could barely choke down half the required amount. After I finished, the endocrinologist kept withdrawing blood every fifteen minutes, then every half-hour, then every hour. The purpose of this test was to measure the level of the hormones that determine how quickly one feels full. The endocrinologist told me that abstainers—anorexics who lose weight by not eating rather than by vomiting or using laxatives—release more of these hormones more often than a normal person and, as a result, feel full sooner. So there is a biological factor to anorexia nervosa. But is it a cause or a result?

The test lasted four long hours. I felt upset because the catheter was in my right arm and I couldn't do any homework.

After lunch, I had to go to the Jean Matheson Pavilion to be interviewed by a psychology student. We sat in a room with a one-way mirror. The rest of the students in the class sat behind the mirror so that they could see me but I couldn't see them. While we talked, the student was very nervous and kept fidgeting. He asked me lots of questions, but I think I disappointed him. I'm not neurotic enough to be any fun! At one point, he asked me if I had any other

40

problems or matters of importance that had become so big they blocked out all other thoughts. "Things you think about all the time," he explained. I said, "You mean obsessions?" The poor fellow was shocked. I think he was embarrassed because he knew his fellow students were listening.

Diane went over my test results with me when I got back to the ward. My levels of calcium, potassium, and other minerals are within the normal range. My heart and liver are fine. The only problems are my fasting glucose level and my chloride level. Fasting glucose means blood sugar level. Everyone has a level of blood sugar that makes the body function at its optimum. Because my blood sugar level is low, I am producing too much insulin in relation to blood sugar. As a result, I feel hungry even after I've just eaten.

The job of chloride is to maintain a balance of the body's electrolytes. Most of my electrolytes are at a normal level. My sodium and potassium levels are slightly off, however. The chloride, therefore, is overworked and is running low.

Another dangerous thing that is happening in my body is that my muscles are losing fluid and becoming weaker. Eventually, when the body doesn't have enough fat, it starts to eat away at muscle, including the heart. Fortunately, my cardiac enzymes have been unaffected. Diane told me that really I am amazingly healthy. She also told me that Karen Carpenter died from a heart attack, resulting from a substance she swallowed in order to make herself vomit.

Yesterday I went to the patients' library. It is very old and has very old books. If I ever want to learn how to tie flies or read the complete translation of Beowulf, I'll know where to go. I thought the library would give me some peace and quiet so that I could do my schoolwork, so I asked Chris to take me there. But it is right across from the veterans' community room and I was forced to listen to an hour of "Under the B, sixteen. Under the G, eight. Bingo!"

SATURDAY, MARCH 19   The weight is finally starting to go on! I'm coming to a dead end with my schoolwork from Cranbrook and desperately need to go to school over at Children's Hospital. That's why I'm trying so hard to gain weight. Chris asked me how I felt about gaining 0.3 kg (that's over half a pound). I said, "Great!" "I find that hard to believe," she said. I know that my thinking is screwed up, but I feel that I've reached a very delicate balance.

41

The insides of my arms are purplish blue with tons of little red dots from all the blood tests I've had. I look like a junkie. It's especially gross because my arms are so skinny and white.

I had a bath this morning in a funny big tub designed for old people. It has special sprayers and knobs for adjusting the water temperature. Of course the door won't lock and there is only a curtain over the doorway to the tub, so I washed in sheer terror and was out in record time.

After supper Diane came in to discuss my test results from the written questions that I answered before coming here. They are graded on something called the Beck scale. A score of 1 to 15 points means you aren't depressed, 16 to 25 means you are mildly depressed, 26 to 35 means you are moderately depressed, and 36 and up means you are severely depressed. While I was filling out the forms, I was thinking to myself, "Ha, ha, aren't they going to be surprised when they find out I'm not depressed at all. These tests are going to show how normal I am." Was I ever in for a shock. I scored 38.

On the eating anxiety test, 0 to 33 points is normal. I thought for sure I'd be well within the norm. I scored 68.

My other scores (for relative craziness, I guess) ranged from 19 to 42, and the norm is 0. Diane didn't beat around the bush. "You are certifiably crazy," she kept saying. "There's no doubt about it—you're nuts." Mom was sitting right there and she went pale. Diane wasn't joking. She said that I will start psychotherapy only after I put on some weight. She says there's no point in starting anything like that now because my concentration level has been impaired. I'm too thin even for treatment. No wonder it's been so much harder to keep up the A's in school. Diane says that after I have some weight on I'll be able to readjust my thinking and really start getting better.

But no one knows how hard it is. You read things and hear everyone say, "Oh yes, it's a real struggle," but I don't think anyone appreciates the actual physical—not to mention mental—discomfort you have to endure. My stomach is full and distended after every meal, and I feel greasy and slimy. I want to wear close-fitting clothes, tie back my hair, and scrub my skin raw. I just pray for strength to take each bite. I try to think of my illness as a physical ailment, one that has a cure. And somehow that's a little easier to accept in a hospital environment. I'm taking responsibility for my problem myself, and that's important. No one is forcing me to eat, but I know what I have to do in order to get what I want and, ultimately, to be normal.

Later I will learn how to handle the parts of the world I'm afraid of. For the time being, though, I'm safe here. Here in the hospital, I don't have to eat things that someone has made just so that I won't hurt that person's feelings. I can choose my own meals and not worry all day about what my mother will cook for supper and how much of it my father will expect me to eat. I don't have to live in terror that someone will find the food I have dropped into my napkin so that I can throw it in the garbage. I don't have to be afraid of not having enough free time to do my homework just because I've been told I must "go out and have fun like most sixteen-year-old girls."

Funny things scare me. Boredom is one of them. Being bored just seems to be such a terrible waste of living time. If I'm forced to waste time when I could be accomplishing something, I feel very frustrated and upset. I feel like a wicked person. I believe in constructive relaxation. When I'm not doing schoolwork, I like to read Dickens, Jane Austen, or the Bible.

After visiting hours today, I went down to the lounge and watched a movie on a rented video. Unknown to me, fortunately, one of the girls on this ward slit her wrists while we were watching the show and a man went right out of his head and was convinced he was having a heart attack. The staff was very good about keeping both incidents hushed up. In fact, I wouldn't have known at all except that Samantha told me. She was sitting at the front desk sorting some papers for Diane and saw the whole thing. The girl lived, and when I saw her she was heavily sedated and being watched around the clock.

SUNDAY, MARCH 20   I now weigh 2.2 pounds more than I did when I came in! But I guess I must be crazy because although it's what I wanted, the increase has made it harder for me to eat. When lunch was sitting there in front of me, I started to shake. It was really scary. I drew the curtains all the way around my bed and tried my best.

I am relieved to know, however, that I can start attending school tomorrow. Diane said that there may be other anorexics attending, but they are under a pediatrician's care at Children's.

43

Finally visiting hours rolled around, and, since my weight was up, Diane let me out on a pass. Mom and I went for a walk in the VanDusen Botanical Gardens. It was the first day of spring, and the weather was beautiful. We talked a lot. Later I said to Mom, "We talk about my problems all the time; what about yours?" She said, "Those are my problems too." Mom is my best friend.

After supper, Diane came in and asked what I had left uneaten on my supper tray. I hate talking about things like that, but I told her. I ate half my turkey, half my vegetables, and one piece of unbuttered brown bread. I did eat all my ice cream, however. Diane calculated the calories I'd lost by not eating all of my supper. She said I had to go downstairs to the cafeteria and buy some food to make up for the lost calories. I could choose what I wanted, so I bought some yogurt and a big banana. I sure didn't want to eat them. That's another law of mine: after dessert, I'm allowed a fifty-calorie snack and then there's not to be another bite of food until breakfast the next morning. But I did eat most of the food and afterwards felt a mixture of pride and disgust.

Diane sure is tough—just what I need. Next she found the pudding and the cheese and crackers I'd put in the fridge. "This is hoarding," she said, "and it's what crazy people do. If you don't eat everything given to you, throw it away or send it back to the kitchen." She was quite upset, and so was I.

MONDAY, MARCH 21   Old Clover snored loud enough to wake the dead last night, and I didn't get much sleep. I'm proud of myself, though; I didn't panic. I just put in my handy earplugs and tried to go to sleep. I didn't even ask for chloral hydrate. Another one of my obsessive fears is that I will be unable to sleep at night. I'm terrified of being the last one awake, of watching the darkness intensify as the minutes tick away. I worry about it all day, and the more uptight I get, the harder it is to sleep. I get depressed at dusk when the day starts to die. Other people say, "Look at the beautiful sunset." But I can't see any beauty in the ending of a day.

My weight was the same this morning, but Chris reluctantly took me over to Children's Hospital anyway. What a place! There are brightly colored murals on all the walls, modern furniture, elevators made to look like little houses--you'd hardly know it's a hospital. I wish I were staying there.

44

The classroom is nice, but the teacher is a supreme witch. I tried to ask a question while she was attempting to figure out one of my algebra problems, and she said, "Listen, you just sit there and be quiet!" Of course my eyes filled up with tears and the whole bit. Sometimes I make myself sick!

But I'm just so frustrated. All this time is going by and I'm doing so little, when I'm used to working hard and having school be an important part of my life. It's terrifying to see my work slip so much. What if I lose my entire grade eleven? Diane says most severe anorexics are here for four months. School will be out by then! Why did this happen?

I did algebra problems with a very nervous volunteer this morning. Then Chris came to escort me back to the ward. I returned in the afternoon and did—or, rather, attempted to do—some social studies. Another anorexic girl in grade eleven was there. She is under a different doctor and says she only has to put on ten pounds. She's very pretty and very nice—also smart. She's lucky to get treatment so early. And because she's in Children's, she has a lovely private room with a carpet, a big color TV, a view, and blue and pink striped curtains and bedspread. I hope to get permission to come and visit her.

When Mom came and we were sitting in my room before supper, a patient in the lounge down the hall started screaming and having hysterics. She kept saying, "Get me out of here!" I was out of my room, and when I heard all the racket I ran like crazy back inside. Mom knew I'd be upset, and she held my hand for a while. I felt OK, but I could tell that Mom was both scared for me and glad that she could walk out of here at night.

Around seven Diane said there was a long-distance call for me. It was Ian. He is probably coming down to Vancouver this weekend to see me. I can't believe it—he spends so much money on me. I feel guilty. I don't even think about him very much, but it's flattering to have his attention. He doesn't seem to care that his girlfriend is in a loony bin. I'm pretty fortunate to have so many concerned friends. It makes me more determined to get this nightmare over with.

After Mom left, I talked to Diane for about an hour—all about her job and research work. She's a nice person, but she made it quite clear that she does not want to become personally involved with any of her patients. I guess she doesn't dare let herself.

45

She gave me a collection of articles about anorexia nervosa, dealing with case histories, methods of treatment, and so on. I found these very upsetting, particularly the one about Karen Carpenter. She looked so awful, and Mom and Diane say that I look just like her — grooves around the mouth, sunken eyes, pasty white face, hair falling out. But I don't think I look quite as bad as she did. I think if I did, I wouldn't dare go out anywhere. People would know right away what was wrong.

There was also a story about a man who was severely anorexic and ran away from this very hospital. Now he lives down on the beach, eating nothing but raw liver. The picture of him made me sick.

I don't think my problem is as serious as these cases. I never got totally neurotic or cut down to a few leaves of lettuce for supper. Mom and Dad would never have put up with that. I certainly never exercised as hard as some of these people did. I used to skip a lot, but I didn't jog five miles a day or anything. I did notice, however, that I sometimes got a burst of energy so strong that it was scary. I would jump around in frenzied activity, and then afterwards my legs would feel kind of rubbery and shaky. The most exercise I can get around here is changing the sheets on my bed and pacing the halls.

TUESDAY, MARCH 22 My weight was up another pound today, and that old terror came back. What if I get to like eating this way? Maybe I won't be able to stop. Maybe I will get fat and ugly and horribly self-indulgent! If I can't control that part of my life, maybe I won't be able to control other things. What if I succumb to the desires of the flesh? I'll be useless — all I'll have left is this self-loathing. There will be nothing else at all.

It's just happening too fast. I wish I could control my weight so that it went up about a quarter of a pound a day. But my body is not a computer and I can't control how much weight goes on. I feel like such a pig because the amount I'm required to gain is so huge.

I went over to the classroom again, did some math, fought with the teacher, and at 11:00 went with Chris to the auditorium for Dr. Sandor's conference with anorexics, bulimics, and their parents. I found out that I can't concentrate properly and lose interest in things because I'm in the starvation-syndrome stage. Once I put on a few more pounds that will improve.

After visiting hours, I talked to Diane for about half an hour. She said they used to have a program for bulimics called flooding. Every day at suppertime the girls were locked in a big room full of food: cream pies, muffins, cake, fries, and so on. Some of the girls gave in to the temptation to binge; others would pour ketchup or something all over the food to keep from eating it. The girls were checked every twenty minutes, and bingers were removed but prevented from vomiting. It sounds like a pretty bizarre way to treat the illness, and I don't know if I agree with it completely. Anyway it had to be discontinued because the expense for all that food became too great.

WEDNESDAY, MARCH 23 My weight was exactly the same this morning—69.1 pounds. I went to school this morning and tried to tolerate the teacher. She bugs me so much! She's always calling us "youngsters." She says, "I have a bone marrow youngster and an isolation youngster to do today." She gets talking and won't let the students or volunteer helpers get a word in edgewise. She thinks she is an expert on every subject, and she's not.

Back on the ward, my escort, Samantha, and I were having a good talk when Stan came in to say goodbye. He's a bulimic-anorexic, and he's been here since January 7. He finally gets to go home today. He has already gained forty-four pounds and has another thirty-five left to go. He is a very nice guy. Like me, Stan craved complete order in his life. He's had to learn how to live all over again. I'm so happy for him!

Samantha is going to send a request to the National Film Board to do a documentary about anorexia and bulimia. It would be shown at all schools for girls about thirteen and up and would show the horrifying results of eating disorders. Some girls seem to think that anorexia nervosa is a chic and interesting new disease. They must know how it can ruin your life! There is so much sensationalism attached to anorexia—it makes me sick.

Samantha was sad today. She had been doing really well, but I guess she binged. Diane doesn't beat around the bush with Samantha either. "Samantha," she says, "did you binge today?"

It makes me so mad the way some people, especially visitors to the ward, seem to think the patients are deaf. I walk down the hall and hear all sorts of interesting comments like, "She's awfully young to be here," or "I wonder what she's in for." My favorite is when some tactful person asks, "What are you in for?"

Mom and Auntie Peggy came to visit tonight. After they left, I felt so sorry for myself that I just sat on the bed and cried. They are free to go wherever they want, and here I am stuck on the psych ward with weird people, blunt nurses, escorts, and my own nagging conscience: "You just ate that because you *wanted* it, you fat pig."

One of the nurses said I have enough flowers to open my own flower shop. It's true. My friends at home have sent daisies, azaleas, mums, carnations, and tulips. My walls are looking less bare too. I made a bunch of posters. One says "MANGE," and another has drawings of girls before and after anorexia nervosa. Mom brought me a ballet poster, and Ian sent a huge poster of Humphrey Bogart. The nurses love it!

THURSDAY, MARCH 24 My weight is up to seventy pounds! Now I'm really scared. Maybe the pounds will just pile on, completely out of my control. I don't know who or what I might turn into. It's just like Dr. Sandor says—I look in the mirror and see a skeleton, but I feel fat. I need to talk with Diane, but she doesn't work today. I am forgetting why I have to do this. Part of me is very happy and proud, but another part is disgusted and repulsed and keeps telling me I'm a gluttonous pig.

Some old guy on the ward named Joe keeps bugging me. He always walks in here yelling "Miss Ardell" and tries to knock on my curtain. He brings me my snack and wants to take away my tray before I'm finished. He keeps returning to check and see if I'm done yet and I can't relax because I never know when he's going to come in. He's really nice, but I don't trust him. He makes me nervous. He and a boy named Tim Wong go jogging together.

When I came back from school, I found that a new girl had been moved into one of the beds in my room. Her name is Mary Lou. She seems nice enough, but her face is all puffy and she's almost bald. Something serious must be wrong with her. She can't have fluorescent lights on around her because she breaks out. In fact, she prefers not to have any lights on at all.

Later I watched a movie in the lounge. Apparently the staff members get quite upset if you don't attend. They don't want people isolating themselves, I guess.

Much as I hate being here and feel guilty for being here, I feel safe

48

and protected. I can choose what activities I do and when I want to do them. I could study all day and all night if I wanted to. No one can forbid me to do the things that are most important to me. And no one looks at me angrily as I struggle to eat my meals or as I pick my food apart and eat it in funny ways. I just can't handle the responsibilities that come with the outside world. I don't know how to be a sixteen-year-old girl. I don't particularly want to be one. I wish I could talk to someone about it, but everyone just says, "Eat and the problems will go away."

FRIDAY, MARCH 25   My weight was the same today—seventy pounds. I spent all afternoon getting ready for Ian to come. At 3:30, I went to the kitchen to get some coffee, and when I came back, there he was. I was pretty happy to see him. He's very handsome, but definitely punk—his hair is cut very short and shaped into a V at the back, and he wears loose, baggy clothes and pins with pictures of the Police on them. I can't believe he came all the way down here just to see me. Can someone besides my family really care about me that much? We talked and I took him on a tour of the place. I asked for a day pass and was refused. Just before Ian left, I looked at him sitting there and I thought, "I think you are cute and funny. I think you are strong and able. I think you are kind, compassionate, and loving. I admire you, and even respect you. But I could never, ever marry you."

I remember meeting Ian at a dance when we were both fourteen. We liked each other right away, but he was always the one who phoned or suggested we do something together. We never formally agreed to "date," but we went places with groups of other friends and enjoyed each other's company. We mostly just joked around and never did have what I consider a deep or serious relationship.

As Ian watched me get skinnier and skinnier and saw my self-confidence dwindle, he encouraged me to eat and even tried to take me out for lunch several times. One day we were sitting together, me weighing about seventy pounds and with what little hair I had left tied back in a thin ponytail. Ian looked good—suntanned and muscular. I said, "Why on earth do you like me, Ian?" He said, "Because I can talk to you. We can actually have conversations. You have depth." I've thought about that statement many times since then, and it has helped me through some rough days.

Right from the time we met, Ian talked about getting married.

49

This made me nervous. Ian didn't have a very happy life, and he seemed to think that we could ride off together into the sunset and live happily ever after, without any problems. I've tried many times to tell Ian that this is just not possible, but I beat around the bush too much and Ian seems to hear only what he wants to hear. What I really need to tell him is that serious commitment is impossible for a girl who has never functioned as an adult. How can I make sound decisions when I weigh less than seventy pounds and do nothing but study all day? I don't know what life is all about.

SATURDAY, MARCH 26   My weight was up to 70.6 pounds today. It scares me to know that I'm getting bigger. The larger I get, the more "there" I am. I'm expected to be normal and I don't know if I can be. Nevertheless, I keep hearing the voice of common sense telling me to keep eating anyway. But I'm afraid to listen to it because another voice says, "You are weakening; you are giving in." I keep trying to reassure myself that I'm not eating for pleasure. I'm eating for purposes that are strictly honorable. I want Mom and Dad to be proud of me. I want them to say, "Maureen never gives us a moment's worry." I want to start living a normal life and to be happy. Yet I'm tortured by endless debate about whether or not I should eat a cookie. A typical inner dialogue:

"Most chocolate-chip cookies have only fifty calories."
"This one is quite big, though."
"Then just have half."
"Maybe I'll have the whole thing and then skip dessert."
"But if I don't eat dessert, I might lose a few points of a pound."
"Good."
"But then I won't be allowed to go to school."
"Well, just set it aside for now and try to eat it later."

I spent the whole morning doing homework. I was told that no patients are allowed in the cafeteria anymore, not even to have coffee with visitors. So I'm stuck in this cell. Even when I want to go a walk, the nurses demand to know exactly where I'm going and why.

Some of the nurses make me sick. They always come in when they haven't got anything better to do and ask the same dumb questions: "How long have you been sick?" "What is your relationship with your father like?" "What did you eat for lunch?" Then

50

they say, "OK, I see," very quietly and in a very understanding voice. That really annoys me because it seems as if some of them get their kicks out of hearing about my problems. They shake their heads slowly and say, "Tsk."

After lunch, Mary Lou had a vision. She saw a knife or something on the ceiling and had to be medicated. I guess she is pretty sick physically and emotionally. I have to sit here in depressing semi-darkness because she can't stand to have the light on. She's on many different kinds of medication and sleeps for most of the day. She needs quiet. Also, she asked that I never speak about religion or let friends speak about it while she's around. She said it's not that she's prejudiced, but she had a "bad experience" with religion a few months ago and it upsets her to hear anything said about it.

Ian came back at two and stayed until eight. We talked and played cards, but we never really had any serious talks. I'm afraid to tell him that I only want to be his friend. I don't want to hurt him and I don't want people to say that I'm just afraid to grow up.

After Ian left, Mom gave me a much needed pep talk and my determination returned. She reassured me that I have loving support from my family and friends and reminded me that I will soon look and feel much better if I keep putting on weight.

"No," she said, "the pounds will not all go on your stomach while the rest of you stays skinny. I promise."

SUNDAY, MARCH 27 Well, what I was determined would never happen has happened. I have lost weight. I let myself act according to how I felt emotionally and physically. My skinny conscience overpowered my reason and told me that I had eaten enough and that if I put in more food I was a glutton who ate for the sheer pleasure of stuffing my face. My body felt full and so I stopped eating. I thought my weight would be OK, but it was down, right back to 69.6 pounds. I lost a pound in one day! I was so ashamed.

Bettina, the little French nurse who sings all the time, let me weigh myself and I couldn't tell her, I just couldn't. I lied. I said my weight was the same as before. Dr. Sandor is right—I am a liar and a cheat. All I can do is eat enough today to bring my weight back up to what it was by tomorrow.

I did math all this morning. This afternoon whenever I closed my eyes I saw rational expressions. I shock all the nurses and cleaning ladies who come in. They say, "Are you still studying?" I'd like to say, "What else can I do?" I'm just glad to have something that keeps my mind occupied.

Mary Lou is still very ill. She must have darkness and silence. I constantly worry about what I say in case it might upset her. The room is so gloomy it starts pressing in on me sometimes. Today when friends were visiting me, one told the other in French not to talk about religion in front of Mary Lou. I said, *"Elle probablement parle le français."*

At lunch time, another friend came in to see me. She was here visiting me and another friend of hers, named Martha, who suddenly went totally out of her mind. She is covered with a terrible rash and talks constantly without making sense. She scared me out of my wits the other night. She was screaming at the top of her voice, "RRRR...The last time! The last time! It was the last time I ever saw him...ALIVE!" She doesn't even recognize her own daughter, who has come all the way from Quebec to visit her. I met Martha today and she seems a bit better. She can string together sentences now, but they are kind of weird. She said to me, "Nice to meet you. I see you have all your teeth." "Yes" was all I could think to say.

After supper the nurses let me go for a little walk outside with Mom. I needed to have a good talk with her. She's very wise. I think in some ways she does me a lot more good than any psychiatrist could because she'll spend all the time in the world with me. I wonder if it's unnatural for a girl to love her mother as much as I do. That was my old shrink's idea. "There's too much love in your family," he said. I'll never believe that.

MONDAY, MARCH 28   This was not a good day, and I am thankful to be looking back on it. My weight was not back up, as I fully expected it to be. I had consumed about twenty-five hundred calories, according to my calculations, including a whole bunch of Smarties while I was playing cards. This time I couldn't go on with the lie. Chris came in to ask about my weight, and I told her it was down "a couple of points." She was mad.

"Look, Maureen," she said, "if you don't watch out, you're going to be flat on your back in bed. You won't even be allowed to do schoolwork or chew gum."

To make matters worse, Dr. Sandor and Diane are away for a

whole week. A young guy with a beard is taking over for Dr. Sandor. But I'm not going to open my heart to a stranger only to have him leave after a week. Then I'll just have to go through it all again. Telling a psychiatrist your problems is like stripping your clothes off in front of a stranger.

This morning was gloomy, dark, and close. Mary Lou wouldn't let me turn the lights on, so I sat in semidarkness feeling sorry for myself and trying to concentrate on algebra. About ten o'clock the nurses moved Martha into our room; they needed hers for the morning in order to do shock treatments. She kept calling me over. "Little girl," she'd whisper.I'd go over and she would start rambling on, not making any sense, but unable to stop: "At least I have the decency to lower my bed it was the funniest book I ever read, really it was, but I was only on page ten when the nurse came in and it wasn't yet time for him to be revealed so I had to brush my teeth bye bye." She also swears and interrupts her daughters. While this was happening on one side, Mary Lou was crying and near hysterics on the other. It was such a pleasant morning!

I finally found out what is wrong with Mary Lou. She got mixed up with a cult group. She was heavily into it when she developed lupus. The treatment includes cortisone, so she's nearly bald and her face is puffy. She was dying but refused to see a doctor because the cult told her that doctors were Satan and hospitals were evil places of torture. She completely isolated herself for a whole year. She refused to talk to her family and never went out or talked to anyone. No wonder talk about the Bible upsets her.

When it became obvious that she was going to die, her family forced her into hospital, where she is finally receiving medical treatment for the lupus and psychiatric treatment for the cultist brainwashing. She is terrified to talk to anyone or go places where more than two people are gathered. She won't even come down to the lounge and watch a movie. Sometimes I can draw her out a bit if I'm careful what I talk about. I usually bring her the meal trays.

A student from Simon Fraser came in and asked me to fill out a whole bunch of questionnaires dealing with body image. I had to look at several photos of girls, some skinny, some fat, and then answer questions about what I think they are like as people. For example, on a scale of 1 to 5, do I think this girl is socially capable? It's ridiculous, really, and I'm sick of being analyzed and questioned.

53

When will these people realize that I can't be stuck into a computer?

The forms took about an hour and a half to complete, and while I was doing them a student from UBC came with more questionnaires for me to fill out. These are for the whole family to answer. That woman is doing research on similarities in the families of anorexics. She is studying twenty-five families with anorexic daughters and twenty-five without anorexic daughters for a control. The sheets will take about two hours to fill out and include questions about how I view my parents and myself and how they view me and themselves. She wants to know about the relationships in anorexic families to see if they have anything in common. But even if she doesn't find any general traits, her research will not have been in vain—a lack of common traits may mean that family relationships do not cause anorexia nervosa.

Mom enjoyed talking to the woman. She seems to need to talk about my illness. But it bothers me to talk about it. It's not exactly that I want to run away from the problem or sweep it under the carpet—I'm just sick of the subject. I don't want anyone to think I'm proud of my behavior. Also, there are so many opinions and ideas about anorexia nervosa, and they all place blame on someone. As Dr. Sandor has said, it doesn't matter why I'm sick. I should just concentrate on getting better.

After supper, Mom and I went to Samantha's room and had a nice long talk. Samantha has just finished a minidocumentary about shock therapy for school. The staff showed her how all the equipment works, but she wasn't allowed to (and had no desire to) witness an actual treatment. Recently shock therapy has been used successfully in the treatment of anorexia nervosa. No one is touching my head!

I won't accept antidepressants if they try to give them to me either. Samantha takes them, but I don't need them. I want to get better by myself.

One of the girls on the ward is here because she tried to commit suicide. She had phoned up her psychiatrist and tried to make an appointment to talk to him, but his secretary said he wasn't feeling well and wouldn't be in that day. That night she tried to commit suicide and was brought here. The next morning she went into the "nourishment center" to get a coffee, and there was her psychiatrist in a nightgown. He hadn't been at work the day before because he was here, receiving shock therapy! What a screwed-up world!

Samantha was very happy today because she has gone five days without a binge, even though she had many powerful urges to binge. She's a special person with so much to give. She gets A's at college and is a talented skater. But bulimia has already ruined a lot for her. She used to skate with Toller Cranston and Karen Magnussen, and she had to give all that up. I just hope bulimia doesn't ruin her writing career. She doesn't deserve to be stuck where she is—a slave to her own body.

TUESDAY, MARCH 29 My weight was up today, and Diane was back. We had a good talk. I really need her. She's firm but encouraging, and I know that she likes me better than Chris does. She is allowing me to go out on day passes from Friday to Tuesday on the condition that my weight either goes up or stays the same on each day. Dad is coming on Thursday of this week, so I really want those passes. I'm nervous, but I know that the facts are simple: I want to go out, so I have to eat.

Tim Wong left today. I'll miss him shuffling in here in his too short pants and his thongs. He would come in three or four times a day and sit down at one of the chairs by my bed. "You speak Engrish?"

"Yes, Tim, do you?"

"Not very wew." One time he pointed to the little cloth butterfly on my flower arrangement and said, "Like you—vewy beautiful." I could have cried when he went shuffling out again.

"OK," he said. "I won't bother you."

Before he left, one of the nurses brought out a hot plate and put it in the kitchen. Tim made a big pot of won-ton soup, which smelled heavenly. All the patients, nurses, and doctors crowded into the tiny kitchen and began eating and talking. Tim stood proudly at the front of the room, smiling from ear to ear: "You want won-ton soup?"

The old guy who always brings my tray and snacks, Joe, is as cheerful as ever. I don't know if he's on a high from his "meds" or what, but he sure is a happy fellow. How can I help but love someone who calls me "beautiful" or "gorgeous" all the time and constantly praises my lovely eyes, hands, and clothes? He seems so normal that I was starting to wonder if he wasn't a patient but a maintenance worker or something. Then one afternoon he came into the kitchen wearing a shirt, a tie, shoes, socks, and a white towel wrapped around his waist, held up by a black leather belt.

"Joe! Where are your pants?" I asked.

He said, "I had a little accident and I didn't think you ladies would mind if I wore this instead of pants."

Samantha says he's a dirty old man and I should try not to be alone with him. He tried to kiss Samantha the other night.

Mary Lou is doing a little better. Yesterday she went down the hall to a "communications" group and was able to talk a little bit. That was really an accomplishment. She was talking to me too. Last night she told me about her disease and how hard it's been for her to be in hospital. I wanted so much to comfort and help her. All I could think to say was, "Things will get better. It's going to be OK." Then I could hear her crying quietly behind her curtain. I wanted so much to go and give her a hug, make her better. But of course I couldn't. I have to leave that up to the staff—I might say the wrong thing. She probably wouldn't have wanted me to anyway. All I can do is try to talk to her when I can and present an optimistic attitude. I feel so sorry for her it hurts.

I asked Diane why it is that since I've been eating so much more I constantly feel dirty. I'm always running to the bathroom to wash my hands, and I brush my teeth about six times a day. She said that because I'm giving up one compulsion I feel I must replace it with another. Part of me must still feel that food is evil and eating is bad because I always have an urge to clean myself. The other day, I had just washed my hands and brushed my teeth before lunch, and when I touched the doorknob to leave the washroom I felt dirty again. That's ridiculous! Maybe I'm crazier than I thought. But Diane says that will go away as I learn to accept my weight gain, although I will always be an extremely tidy person.

About ten-thirty last night, we were all gathered in the lounge watching the final episode of *The Thorn Birds*. I was sitting beside the fire escape. Suddenly I looked up and was shocked to see a very ugly man's face looking in at us all in our pajamas. One of the girls stood up and switched off the TV. "Don't let him in!" she hissed. There were two men out there. They were drunk, I guess, and somehow had climbed in and got stuck on our fire escape. We couldn't open the door because the silent alarm would go off. Finally, one of the nurses called security and two official-looking men came up and let them in. "Far out," one of the intruders said as they trudged through our ward, having a good look at us all in our pajamas and oversized hospital dressing gowns.

At three today Mom came for a little conference with Diane. Diane told her not to bug me to eat on the weekend or say anything about it because I'll be the one who suffers if I don't eat. I think that's a good plan. Mom doesn't usually pressure me but just reminds me of the need to eat lots and gets depressed when I don't.

Dad arrived today. I was so happy to see him!

THURSDAY, APRIL 7 The day passes last week went OK. We went shopping and visiting, and I ate most of my meals here at the hospital. I also slept here, while Mom and Dad stayed at Auntie Peggy's. My weight was OK every day except this past Tuesday, so I lost one of my day passes and felt pretty lonely. I spent the day doing schoolwork. Right now I'm off on "Spring Break," but I want to keep studying and keep up with all the work.

I know now that I could never be a nurse. Every day I sit and listen to the nurses caring for the men who have had strokes or lost their minds. I admire the nurses and feel ashamed of myself because I find those ancient men disgusting. One of them moans and cries all day. His moaning wakes me up around six in the morning. "AARRRGGG!" he cries.

"What's wrong with Stan, Judy?" one nurse asks.

"He wants to go on the toilet," Judy answers.

Every evening the nurses help the old people fill out their menus: prune juice, All-Bran, digestive biscuits. A typical conversation (only the nurse can be heard because she has to shout):

"Do you want boiled cabbage or buttered spinach?"

"But you haven't had vegetables all day!"

"Cream and sugar?"

"Butter? But you have no bread."

One old guy who has had a stroke always comes into my room. His name is Doug, and he sits in his wheelchair wearing a bright red jogging suit. He propels himself forward by walking his feet. He says and does ridiculous things, but it's sad because he's so serious about them. This morning I saw him repeatedly jabbing his French toast with a knife held in his fist. He had a look of such intense concentration on his face, as if it were very important to impale this particular specimen of food.

He loves to come into my room during the day, but he knows he must do it on the sly because the nurses get mad at him. But often, even when I have the curtain drawn around my bed, I look down and see bright red legs moving frantically, and I know Doug has come for a visit. He then tries to open the curtains, puffing and panting and getting lost in the folds. Finally he gets them open and stares at me for a while. Then he says something like, "Where the hell is the occupational therapy group?"

Last week when my aunt was visiting, Doug sat in his room across the hall and stared into my room. Then he started making eyes and waving frantically at my aunt. "I think I have a friend," she said. Sure enough, before long he was in the room checking out the new chick.

But what he really loves to do is wheel himself in right when I'm in the middle of an important discussion with Dr. Sandor. I find it impossible to continue with a bright red old man goggling up at me.

And Doug can never quite maneuver his way out of the room. I usually go and turn his chair around and wheel him back out to the hall. "Thanks," he says. "Maybe I can do as much for you one day."

Joe finally got to go home, and I never did find out what was wrong with him. Now there's no one to make a big fuss over me and tell me I have pretty eyes. There's no one in the kitchen at night eating cold French fries and milk. I'm going to miss him. (And I don't believe he's a dirty old man.)

On Tuesday afternoon, I went to my group therapy meeting at the Jean Matheson Pavilion. There were five girls there, including me. One girl is new. Her name is Vanessa, and I think she's very beautiful. She's not cute — more sexy. Anyway, she's in town to talk to Dr. Sandor because she's five foot seven and weighs 98 pounds. She used to be a chubby 147 pounds but now is an anorexic-bulimic. She diets, vomits, and takes laxatives. She won't admit she's anorexic, though. She kept saying, "I'm not anorexic. I'm the fattest one in here." It was almost as if she were ashamed that she didn't look like a skeleton, like the rest of us.

The meeting was pretty good. We discussed body image and how our society constantly bombards us with the idea that thin is beautiful. Yet everywhere you look there are pictures and ads for every kind of food and drink you can think of. No wonder we are all mixed up. It's good to be reminded that I'm not the only one who has a strange attitude toward food. All of us are in the same boat.

Still, I don't feel I have much in common with the rest of the girls in the group. Most of them hate their parents and openly admit they are trying to hurt them. I keep saying I don't feel this way at all and honestly don't know why I got anorexia nervosa. Dr. Sandor maintains that I'm vain and want the "perfect" body.

Anyway, I said to him that I really wish the problem were more concrete and clear-cut so I could fight against it better. I find it hard to be constantly battling my own mind, praising and condemning myself for the same things. If I could just get rid of the ambivalence. Dr. Sandor said, "I'll give you something concrete to do." The next day he came into my room and said, "Vanity, vanity; all is vanity." He told me to find where this quote is from in the Bible. I knew it was in Ecclesiastes. I did a long series of notes for Dr. Sandor about Ecclesiastes. He knows a lot about the Bible himself—I suppose any really well educated person does—and likes to quiz me. "What is the Septuagint?" he asks. Then he tells the other girls, "Maureen wants to be a preacher and she's very good. But you can't be a preacher without a body."

On Tuesday night, Mom went to a support group for family and friends of people on the psych ward. While the group discussed the heartbreak involved in raising or being married to a loony, Diane took me to a private office upstairs for a talk. It really did me a lot of good and gave me some insights into my own personality. I think I learned more about myself in that hour and a half than in the rest of my teenage life.

She told me about certain protective screens I put up. The biggest of these screens is, of course, the anorexia. Perhaps I'm afraid to find out what I am really like as an adult. Connected to this is the screen of isolation. Diane says I'm afraid to go out and be with people besides my parents because they might say something that I wouldn't know how to handle. To me, the risk just isn't worth it—I'd rather stay home. Someone might comment on my thin hair or suggest that we go out for pizza. But I'm also afraid my parents will make me eat, so I end up being alone as much as I can. And to prevent me from thinking about my eating problem, I drown myself in schoolwork—another screen.

Diane told me some other things that certainly didn't make me feel good about myself, but they were things that had to be said. For example, she said that although having anorexia nervosa is a painful experience, it's hard to give up. Even though I am hurting my family, I'm not yet willing to give up my behavior. I still very much want to be this way, and one of the most important steps to recovery is wanting to be normal. I often equate being normal with being average, and I want to believe that I'm special. But maybe I can learn to be special in a productive rather than a destructive way. Diane also said that I'm giving up a very big part of my life, one I'm clinging to for protection, and that I had better have something good to replace it with or my recovery won't be permanent.

I was able to really open up to Diane and tell her things I never admitted before. Things like how I often time myself to make sure that five full minutes pass between each bite of food. And how I feel like a bad person if I eat at a faster rate. Or the way I stash uneaten food in my pockets and behind furniture in order to dispose of it later when no one is looking. I also told Diane about the times I think of suicide. I don't think I would ever kill myself, but sometimes when I'm walking beside a busy street I wonder how it would feel if a car or truck ran into me and ripped me right up. If I were lucky, the pain probably wouldn't last that long. But that would be taking the easy way out, and I don't want it ever to be said that I was a cop-out.

Diane says I have to start thinking seriously about my own future and start making decisions and taking responsibility for myself. I have to be responsible enough to take care of my own body and mind. I have the ability to stop doing crazy things and thinking crazy thoughts, so I have to do it. No one else can do it for me.

I am behind others my age. My estrogen level is very low, so I'm physiologically two or three years behind my contemporaries. But Diane says I can catch up. I will have to condense my whole adolescence into a few months, since I'm still a prepubertal child. And I'll still have to go through a rebellious stage, like all normal teens.

I was glad to have a talk with Diane because I was suffering a great deal of mental anguish after have consumed over eighteen hundred calories today. My stomach feels very bloated.

FRIDAY, APRIL 8   Well, my weight was up 0.3 kg this morning—that's over half a pound. That's comfortable—it's not going up frighteningly fast, but it's good to see some results after all the agony I suffered yesterday.

We had a meeting here in my room with Dr. Sandor from 9:30 to 10:00. It was bulimics and me. I really don't feel that we have anything in common. Our problems are so different. It makes me sick to even think about bulimia. But Dr. Sandor insists that we are all after the same thing—a perfect body. I didn't really think I thought about my body or my shape very much. But Dr. Sandor says we all have a desperate need to be slim. He said he once took a survey and 20 percent of anorexic girls would rather be dead than fat. He also pointed out to me that the magazine pictures I decorated my room with are all of gorgeous models with fantastic figures and long slim legs. I felt pretty sheepish. I never really realized that before.

Anyway, Dr. Sandor said Vanessa is going to be admitted soon. I wish there were another abstainer, but Vanessa is mostly bulimic.

SATURDAY, APRIL 9   I am very lonely tonight. Just about everyone has gone home on weekend passes, and I feel very depressed in this dark room. Mary Lou won't let me have the door or window open, or the lights or radio on. She eats in the kitchen now. The staff is trying to get her out more. But she resists all their efforts. She gets mad when they make her go to the Communication I or "skills" group; yet in the same breath she complains that there is nothing to do. Last night her mom came and brought her a beautiful flower arrangement. Mary Lou started screaming, "I don't want them, I don't want them! They'll die!" It's so hard to know when she's just feeling sorry for herself and when she's really feeling mental anguish. How far do you push? Mom says that a certain amount of will enters into combatting all mental illness, that a person must honestly have the desire to get better. But I guess no one knows all the answers.

Last night I went into the kitchen for some milk and Jeff was there. He's a young man who has been here quite a while. He is short and kind of fat and has a red beard. He looks like Fred Flintstone in a bathrobe. He also speaks very slowly, kind of shuffles along, and says a lot of irrelevant and inappropriate things. But he's sweet. "How's the schoolwork coming?" he always asks. Last night he seemed upset. "They're kicking me out of here soon."

"Isn't that nice!" I said. "I bet you'll be glad to get home."

"I don't think I'm ready yet."

"Oh . . . well, still, it'll be nice to be out of here, won't it?" I said.

"Yeah. Next time I try to commit suicide I think I'll jump off of something." Then he was silent.

"Goodnight, Jeff," I said.

"G'night, Maureen."

I hope I feel more confident than that when I finally go home. I don't think anyone is ever ready to go back into that mean old world, but you have to just jump in and try as hard as you can. All of us on this ward are "sinkers," but some of us will learn and maybe one day we'll be able to swim.

Ian phoned last night, and I talked to him for half an hour. He lives in an apartment now, with his best friend. He and his parents aren't talking. He works full time and makes good money. He seems to be happy, but I have a feeling it won't last.

MONDAY, APRIL 11   This morning my weight was up by almost a quarter of a pound, so I was allowed to go out for the day. Last night I went down to the cafeteria and bought a bunch of things for lunch today. I put them in a brown paper bag and put it in the fridge. Then I went to bed. This morning the bag was on my table, empty, with a note taped to the side: "Maureen, you have been dehoarded, Diane." I was furious and had to go down to the cafeteria and buy all that stuff over again. I left Diane a note at the nurses' station: "You owe me a lunch! That was *not* a hoard."

Everything I do is suspect. I say, "That's a pretty girl." The non-anorexics say, "Anorexics are too body conscious." I say, "I'll bring Mary Lou her supper tray." They say, "You are obsessed with food." I say, "I feel nauseated." They say, "You just don't want to eat." I hope I don't get stomach flu and throw up. They might say I was turning bulimic!

I'm sick of this place and of snippy nurses, nosy nurses, questions, old men, and stuffy rooms with windows that only open two inches (you never know — I might jump out). I want to go swimming and have a bubble bath and not have to sign in and out every time I go somewhere. I want to rely on myself more. I want to be *normal*! Does that mean I'm ready to eat?

TUESDAY, APRIL 12   Today was a very bad day. Any novelty that made being here interesting has worn off. I hate it and feel bitter.

To start with, Mary Lou and I had to go to the kitchen while our room was cleaned. She proceeded to stagger around the kitchen and then pass out, hitting her head on the fridge. I ran and got the doctor for help.

Then an escort took me to the classroom, but I could not concentrate at all. It was terrifying to sit there and not be able to get a thing done. I kept thinking about my weight. It had been up another half a pound and I was pleased until I remembered that Dr. Sandor said it was important not to gain very fast. If I keep going up by half a pound or so every day, I'll gain much more than two pounds a week. Yet if I cut down on my calories at all, I might lose. I was consumed by a raging nausea. I just couldn't eat all day.

And that stupid ugly teacher who does me more harm than good kept flitting in and out in her old-lady white leather shoes — click, click, click. "How are we doing? Any foreseeable problems?" All the typical teacher jargon. "We're looking at a question of . . ."

Plus the classroom is full of very sick little kids. There are bald kindergarteners, paralyzed grade threes, a dwarf in grade ten, and more. It's all very depressing and makes concentration difficult. Computerized i.v.'s are always beeping, nurses are rushing in and out, babies are always howling, and, to top it all off, the kindergarteners are enthusiastically learning all about Peter Rabbit while I try to solve quadratic equations.

The elementary school teacher yelled at me because I didn't answer the phone. "Student! Student!" she said. "Will you kindly answer it next time?"

My so-called teacher is always peeing her pants to get me out of there by 11:30. But if I try to leave a little earlier (if the escort is early), I face the wrath of God. Yesterday she was in a frenzy to be off to her "bone marrow youngster" and at 11:30 told me to phone my ward and remind the clerk about the escort.

"You'll just have to wait, Maureen. They are all in a very important meeting right now," the ward clerk informed me.

I relayed the information to the teacher. She turned to a volunteer tutor: "Mark, I can't leave this child alone. Would you sit with her until the escort comes, please?"

Does she think I'm going to rush out and make myself vomit? My face turned red in anger. I'm sixteen! How old does she think I am?

But I didn't know what humiliation was yet. When I finally got back to the ward, Chris approached me. "I went through your drawers this morning, Maureen, and found far too much food stored there. Now I'd like you to put it all in the kitchen, please."

Creep that I am, I meekly agreed. "Oh yes, Chris, right away Chris." But inside I was boiling with rage. How dare she touch my things! How dare she look at my personal belongings! Can't they leave me any dignity at all? I found out later that she also went through my duffel bag.

I just couldn't handle lunch. I felt so sick to my stomach that I gave up. I got out of going back to the school room in the afternoon because I had a group therapy meeting at 3:30. I could have gone, but I just couldn't face that bag again. This afternoon was the worst I've had since coming here. I just couldn't get any work done at all. Everything seemed so dark, and I felt so lonely. Minutes dragged by like hours.

It was beautiful outside—the sky was so blue. I looked out my window and watched spring slip away. It seemed somehow symbolic—like I was watching my youth go by too. My heart hurt. I kept thinking, "How did I get here? What am I doing here?" But I couldn't cry. I was too sad for tears.

The group therapy meeting was OK, although rather depressing. Dr. Sandor was telling us about all the fun he had as a youth. Evidently he was very active and healthy. He said that we could be like that too, but we are wasting the best years of our lives. I know that and am afraid that there's no hope for me. I've missed the boat and it's not coming back just to pick me up.

WEDNESDAY, APRIL 13   When I got back to my room yesterday afternoon, it was after five and my poor mom had been waiting there for an hour. She tried to cheer me up, but instead I got her depressed too. All I could do was play cards. I couldn't concentrate on a single thing. We played cards all evening. When night came and visiting hours were over, I could feel a big panic coming on. I tried to calm myself after Mom left. Nothing else bad could possibly happen, could it? I decided to watch some TV. The set was broken. I decided to have a nice long bath. The maintenance crew had shut off the water. I went to bed and tried to read. I couldn't retain a thing. I

64

finally fell asleep with the light on but woke up fifteen minutes later to the sound of an old man's groaning and an old woman's snoring. I had a very disturbed and restless sleep, knowing my weight would be down. I hate this place. But not as much as I hate myself.

Today all my hard work, all my torturous suffering, has gone right down the drain. Just because of one day of nausea, my weight plummeted to seventy-one pounds. I lost a whole pound—not much for a normal person, but a great deal to an anorexic.

They wouldn't let me out of bed this morning because the fire alarm had gone off, unaccountably, and they had to "keep track of everyone." I hardly think this necessitates lying flat on one's back.

I talked to Dr. Sandor at 10:00. He says I have lanugo—a layer of fine, dark hair that grows all over an anorexic's body to help maintain body heat. I just thought I had hairy arms—I didn't know it was lanugo.

Clover went home for good, although rumor has it that the doctors just gave up on her. I hope they don't give up on me.

I got to go outside for a short walk before supper (with an escort, of course). It was exhilarating. I start to feel claustrophobic sitting here all day.

Mostly, though, I just feel disgusted with myself. But I feel disgusted when I gain weight too. I'm pretty well trapped, I guess.

After dinner (for some reason, I can't bring myself to say the words "food," "breakfast," or "supper" anymore—more of my silly rules), I got some visitors. The family that Mom is staying with came to see me. I think I handled the situation OK. The conversation flowed quite freely, and I didn't say anything too stupid or get stuck for words.

THURSDAY, APRIL 14 Around nine o'clock last night a new patient came in to take Clover's place. Her name is Lynn. She seems very nice and, much to my relief, doesn't snore.

I am in a drugged stupor and can barely write this. They've put me on an antidepressant, despite the fact that I don't feel chronically depressed.

This morning I was called into the conference room. Dr. Sandor didn't believe that I have been very nauseated. He said, "You had diarrhea, right? That's what they all say." Then he said he was going to put me on an antidepressant called Elavil, 25 mg three times a day. Right in front of everybody, my eyes filled up with tears. I was so ashamed. Diane said, "We're just giving you a little help." Dr. Sandor said, "I like you. I'd adopt you if I could."

I don't want their stupid pills. I just want to be me. Not me plus a pill.

After that I went off to school and kept reasonably busy. When I got back Diane gave me a very tiny pink pill. While I was eating lunch I began to feel the effects of the pill. I suddenly noticed that I couldn't really taste the food and that there was a terrible taste in my mouth. I ignored these signs, thinking I was just tired. Then when I tried to make the good copy of an essay I'd written, I found that my eyes were very heavy and wouldn't focus properly. I kept losing my place on the page. Still I didn't clue in. "I shouldn't have read so late at night," I kept thinking.

Finally I just couldn't write anymore. I lay down on the bed, thinking I'd just read for a minute. When I opened my eyes, an hour and a half had gone by! I felt as if I were in a dream as I staggered down to the nurses' station, nearly bumping into the walls as I went. I asked Diane if the pills were making me this way. "Oh yes," she said. "You'll feel like that for the next three or four days."

They hadn't even warned me! They said the only side effect would be a dry mouth. I stumbled back to bed and slept for another hour and a half. When I finally woke up, there were some visitors in my room—some people Mom had met and asked to visit me. But I just couldn't talk. I couldn't even sit up. I got a coffee and fell asleep again with it in my hand. The pills were making me depressed. When Mom came I was lying there with glazed eyes and tears coursing down my cheeks. "Great antidepressant pill," she said.

FRIDAY, APRIL 15   Last night I slept like a stone. Then this morning I had another pill at eight. It made a ghastly sour taste in my mouth. I couldn't go to school. I couldn't do any homework. I couldn't think.

Around nine-thirty Chris came in and said I could have a weekend pass—starting this morning. The only reason I got it was so that Chris could have the weekend off. If all her patients are out on pass, she doesn't have to work. I phoned Mom and she came right down on the bus. I was in a total daze—a sort of walking zombie—but we went shopping and had a great time. We phoned Auntie Peggy to come and pick us up and then went and had lunch. This evening I broke out in a terrible itchy rash all over my body. Mom phoned the hospital and was told I should stop taking the pills. The last two days are still a blur.

MONDAY, APRIL 18   I didn't lose any weight over the weekend! In fact, I gained two-thirds of a pound. I told Diane about it, and she said I'm doing really well and can go out next weekend too.

When I was ready to leave for school Diane said I could start going without an escort now. So, after a good morning at school, I was shocked to find Chris there at 11:30. When I told her that Diane said I could start going to school by myself, Chris looked extremely annoyed. "That was just for this morning," she said. As we were getting on the elevator she said, "You have been moved."

I was totally shocked. "Why?"

I could tell that she was very angry. "You're probably sick of being here, but we're sick of you too. You aren't making any progress and we want you right by the nurses' station where we can keep an eye on you. You will room with April Kent."

"Oh, I don't know her."

Chris got really mad then. "Of course you don't know her. You isolate yourself all the time and won't talk to anyone! And you still hide away behind a curtain to eat."

I sounded like a whiny kid. "But Diane said I wasn't ready to start eating with the others," I protested.

That's when she really exploded. "I am your primary nurse, not Diane, and I'm telling you to do it from now on. And I wish you'd look at me when I speak to you. It's very annoying!"

She took me into my new room. Everything had been carelessly thrown onto the bed, and several of my posters were torn. I didn't want to cry, but I did. I don't think I've ever hurt as much as I did then.

My new room is small, with just two beds, and they are very close together. I have the bed closest to the door, so I can't curtain my section off and I can't see out the window. April scares me. About once every hour she comes into my room, flings herself onto the bed, and starts writhing around, kicking and flailing her arms, throwing things, punching the mattress, moaning, and shaking uncontrollably. This fit lasts from fifteen minutes to an hour, and I can't get away. She is a very big woman and makes a lot of noise.

I don't know how much of this I can take. Sometimes I wish I could die.

Dr. Sandor wanted to see me at 1:30. He didn't say much, as usual, except that I can't be a very spiritual person if I am that concerned about my appearance. I didn't even bother to try telling him that I'd be willing to be hideously ugly if it meant getting out of here. He wouldn't believe me anyway. He said I would be put on a new antidepressant drug called Anafranil. I asked him if he would put me on bed rest if my weight dropped. He didn't even hesitate. "No," he said.

After I calmed down a little, I fixed up my new room. I was just beginning to feel OK, like I might survive, when that snippy little French nurse came in and started nagging me. "Did you eat your snack?" She doesn't know anything about my problem and should just butt out of my life. It was all just too much and I started crying and told her to leave me alone. She got a very smug look on her face as if to say, "See, I knew it. You're nuts!"

TUESDAY, APRIL 19   Today is Mom and Dad's twenty-first anniversary. It's the first one they've ever spent apart.

I had group therapy at 3:30. Vanessa and I and six other girls were there. All of them are beautiful; they could all be models if they didn't look so much like skeletons. Vanessa is on the acute wing, just waiting for a bed here. Dr. Sandor said we can be roomies! Vanessa seems quite nice, but kind of wild. She used to be on drugs and she smokes. But I think that just being with someone my own age who understands my problem (and doesn't snore) will be a big help.

I also met a recovered anorexic today. Her name is Sally and she is just beautiful. She recovered in a Halifax hospital and is now totally cured. I want to follow her example. She tells me that her hair fell out just as badly as mine when she was sick. But now she's got thick, healthy blond hair. I hope mine will thicken up too. I've lost about a third of it.

Tiffany, the woman anorexic at group therapy, worries that her little daughter may become anorexic since 6 percent of the anorexics who are mothers raise anorexic children. We also talked about health food, and I found it interesting that everyone but me had a mother who was heavily into health foods.

WEDNESDAY, APRIL 20 I hit the big 33 kg this morning. That's 72.8 pounds. I feel OK about it. Maybe I'm finally on the way.

Dr. Sandor came to see me this morning, but we couldn't talk in my room because April was having another anxiety attack. So we went into Samantha's room. Dr. Sandor is a genius. He knows everything about everything. He said that I could get better if I could learn to appreciate myself. Several of the anorexics he treats are masochistic. They burn or cut themselves. I said, "I'm not masochistic!" He said, "Don't tell me you don't fantasize about inflicting pain on yourself." Brother! What do they think I am? But I'm getting to really like Dr. Sandor. He truly cares about each one of his patients.

I went to school, but the Anafranil made me so drowsy I came back to the ward at eleven and slept until noon. I was also very tired because April's snoring had kept me awake half the night. Finally I went and asked the night nurse if I could sleep in the treatment room. She said no. But a different nurse let me sleep on an empty bed.

April is a very unhappy woman. She hasn't lived at home for the past eleven months. The other night she brought the phone into our room while Mom and I were playing cards, and it was heartbreaking listening to her talk to her kids. Now she's having marital problems too. Any situation that's even a little stressful sends her into another anxiety attack. She sweats so hard she soaks the bed. The last two mornings I've had to run and get a nurse to medicate her.

On the brighter side, though, Mary Lou has been released. I hope she's OK. Last night Diane took Mary Lou and me out to celebrate. We went to Baskin-Robbins and had an ice cream. I ate the whole thing!

THURSDAY, APRIL 21 My weight was up another point of a kilogram. I think I just might be getting better. Today has to be really good because if my weight isn't up tomorrow I don't get my weekend pass. I'll do it, though. I'm eating with the others and everything.

The Anafranil is making me so tired. I slept from 11:00 A.M. until noon today and would have slept right through lunch if the nurse hadn't wakened me. Then I slept from 2:30 to 4:00 and would have kept sleeping if Mom and Dad hadn't come on time. It is such a deep sleep, and I say such stupid, incoherent things when they wake me up. The medication also makes me shake, and occasionally my stomach muscles involuntarily tense up. I don't like it at all.

Dad got into town last night, and after supper today Diane made a special trip to talk to the three of us, even though it wasn't her night to work. We had an excellent discussion and really got some things out in the open. I fought back my urge to just smooth things over and said how I really felt. Dad said some interesting things too. He admitted that he can't stand to sit at the table and watch me pick away at my food. He always gets up and leaves as soon as he's finished eating. I thought he just didn't want to talk to me, but the truth is that it hurts him to watch me eat that way. I eat too little and too slowly.

Dad also said that at times when he is telling me to eat more of a certain thing, I look at him with hatred. I said that I don't hate him, but I hate the person he wants me to be. I hate what he is trying to make me do.

Diane knows just what to say. She said Dad and I don't know each other well enough and we have to talk and tell each other what we really think. I didn't realize how much I bottle things up. And this trait has contributed to my anorexia. Instead of telling my father that I was angry about something he had said or done, I would just keep quiet but eat less. I was not consciously trying to punish or hurt my parents, but I guess it turned out that way.

I also realized last night how worried and upset Mom and Dad have been while I tried to pretend there was nothing wrong. They stood by helplessly watching their daughter starve herself to death. Dad got upset while we were talking. He said, "I can't stand to watch her eat. She picks and pokes at everything. When you eat a cookie, you take a bite of the damn thing!"

Diane said, "No, *you* take a bite of the damn thing — she doesn't."

I think this applies to other aspects of life too. Just because my dad, whom I fear and respect, is a "cookie biter" doesn't mean I have to be one too. Dad really likes Diane.

FRIDAY, APRIL 22   Well, I've hit 73.6 pounds — I get my weekend pass! I went to school for an hour because I had to show Rob how to get there. Rob is a new boy on the ward. He's my age and also extremely good-looking. I don't know what's wrong with him, but he seems perfectly normal. I felt pretty shy and ugly (there's a zit on my chin), but I managed to talk to him OK.

Mom and Dad picked me up and we went shopping. We had lunch at Woodward's, and I was OK because I've been there before and know what to expect.

Then we drove down to Robson Street, which is lined with all kinds of neat import and specialty shops. I would have really enjoyed it if the Anafranil hadn't been making me so sick. My teeth kept clenching and I was practically asleep on my feet. For a minute, I felt as if I were going to swallow my tongue, but then the feeling went away. I can't wait to go off these pills.

TUESDAY, APRIL 26   Depression city! My weight was down today. I hate this place! I want to be better right now. I feel as if I'm disappointing and hurting everybody. Why aren't the pounds going on? I think I'm going to be here for months, and I feel so guilty. I feel like a selfish, self-centered, vain little rat. And I have such a wonderful family and so many good friends. I don't deserve them all.

We had another really good group therapy session. I'm getting to know and like the girls, and we all help each other. I can't wait until Vanessa comes. I'm worried about her. She refuses to consume more than eight hundred calories a day and flatly says she will never gain the four pounds Dr. Sandor wants her to gain. She had a binge on Sunday (she was away all weekend and the snacks piled up) and then simply flexed her stomach muscles and brought it all up.

Sally, my recovered anorexic friend, came up to my room for a visit. Mom and Sally went to the hospital cafeteria together for supper. Mom talks Sally's ear off because she wants to know all about her successful recovery. Mom was very impressed when Sally ate a chocolate bar. "I know you can do that some day," she said to me.

THURSDAY, APRIL 28   I sure wish I could be out under that gorgeous blue sky. I can feel that the time for Mom to leave me is getting close. The idea of that scares me. But at the same time I'm excited too. Maybe I can be independent. Maybe that's what I need. I have lots of friends here now. Maybe it's time I stopped clinging to "Mommy."

There are lots of new people here. The turnover is fairly constant—

just when I'm getting to know somebody, she leaves and a new person comes in.

April is having a really rough time of it. Her anxiety attacks are more frequent and more severe. The worst part is that family problems are developing as a result. Her husband and kids don't know how to cope with the problem. Her husband has failed to show up for the last two family therapy meetings. April talks about her kids a lot. She loves them so much and feels guilty about not being at home with them. Something as minor as phoning her family sets her off on another attack. She gnaws her fist and pounds on the bed. Today she had to have an injection, and the sides of her bed were put up so she wouldn't hurt herself. It all made me feel upset too.

There's a new woman on the ward — her name is Maybelle — and she's a real character. She's about sixty-five and I'd say maybe four feet ten at the tallest. She is diabetic and can't talk very well. She shuffles along the halls wearing a skirt down to her ankles, shocking red lipstick, and a wig that she puts on backwards and never combs. Everything she does is in exaggerated slow motion. She's always trying to cheat on her diet and has seizures from time to time. She smokes like a chimney. This morning I nearly burst out laughing when Diane said to her, "Perhaps I could suggest that you wash your face, dear, because you *do* have breakfast on it" and Maybelle responded, "No, no, that's from lunch yesterday."

Today was such a good, good day! I had two breakthroughs. I ate shepherd's pie at lunch, and I broke my law about not eating desserts before 6:00 P.M. and actually had a brownie at 3:30. I'm so happy and proud of myself because at last I can see progress. Now I can really feel myself getting better. I *am* going to beat this thing — I've already come so far. Diane says I get a pass this weekend, and I know my weight will be up. We are going to have a gas — and the weatherman predicts an absolutely gorgeous weekend. The only thing bothering me today is this silly Anafranil. I still sleep away two-thirds of the day and this twitching business can be extremely embarrassing. Plus I feel like such a fool when my voice shakes.

FRIDAY, APRIL 29   How can one person take this much hurt? How can I handle it? I wish I'd never been born because then I wouldn't have to suffer like this. I think my heart is a stone and it's going to fall out on the floor. How come tears don't help? Tears are just a by-product of sadness. They have no healing power. I am so miserable, it hurts, it just hurts all over.

I don't understand how my weight could possibly have gone down. I tried so hard, and I was sure it would be at least 33.7 kg — or about seventy-four pounds — but it was only 33 kg — not quite seventy-three pounds. I was so proud and happy yesterday. It doesn't seem fair. How can I stay in this prison all weekend? The sunlight and blue sky seem to be mocking me — I can only look out the glass and wish I were outside. I've missed so much of my life already; now I'm missing more.

I might not even get to go Saturday or Sunday either. I cried on the cleaning lady's shoulder, and she said, "Wrap the doctor around your little finger, love." Fat chance.

Dr. Sandor and Diane came in to see me at 10:30 this morning. He felt bad, I could tell, but he couldn't let me go. He said my Anafranil will be doubled. I was so ashamed. I couldn't look at him and I went and cried again. Stupid humiliating tears! Dr. Sandor said I could have a pass tomorrow if my weight is up. As he left, he asked, "Do you still like me?" I just nodded.

I have 25 mg of Anafranil at 8:00 A.M., 50 mg at 5:00, and 75 g at bedtime. I can't stand it! Diane says I'll probably feel hung over in the morning. I think I may never wake up but just sleep the rest of my life away. Ha! I wouldn't be able to eat then, would I? Dr. Sandor said that if I try to fool them and not take my Anafranil, I'll have to have injections. "And," he said, "considering the size of your bum, I don't think that would be too nice." You know you've really hit rock bottom when you find yourself discussing your bum size with a bald shrink.

SATURDAY, APRIL 30   I am sitting here listening to the birds chirping outside. The room is flooded with light. It's a special kind of light that comes with a clear spring morning. "Not a cloud in the sky," everyone keeps saying. "What a beautiful day." Occasionally my body jumps, like a giant hiccup. It's the Anafranil. My hands are shaking. It's hard to write.

Apparently my body doesn't realize that it was fed twenty-nine hundred calories yesterday (pie, ice cream, juice with Caloreen, extra meat, cake).

"You aren't doing too well, are you?" the nurse said when she weighed me at six this morning. "No pass for you."

Why am I being punished when I'm trying so hard to do what's right? Why am I still losing weight? Something inside me keeps saying, "You are a bad, wicked girl." But I'm not bad! I'm trying my very hardest to do what's right. This isn't much of a life. I have thought about suicide, but I know I won't do it. Besides, how could I? They take precautions in the psych ward. The windows only open halfway, and there are no knives lying around. I don't want to die, but I don't want to go on living like this either. I'm trying to retain my sense of humor. Mom says that's important. But it is getting kind of discouraging. What if they just give up on me and throw me back out into the world? I'm scared.

Just about everybody has gone home. The ward is pretty lonely. This morning Maybelle and I were the only ones in the lounge for breakfast. She looked at me with an eggy face for a long time. Then she said, "I love you." I paused and then said, "That's nice."

An interesting thing I've noticed lately is that no one around here can simply say, "The trays are here," or "It's suppertime." The nurses have a whole list of little phrases, like "Soup's on" and "Chuck wagon's in."

I spent the entire day doing schoolwork. It was tiring and depressing. The place was deserted except for Maybelle and me and the new fellow, who has to have one-on-one nursing so he doesn't try to kill himself. I talked Diane into letting me eat with Mom in the cafeteria. I did really well. I didn't think I could do it, but I ate the whole meal. There were tears in Mom's eyes when she looked at my plate. I know I'm starting to get better because I find myself thinking about things from Mom's point of view.

At night we all watched *The Blues Brothers* and had a good laugh. Maybelle laughed uproariously at inappropriate places and I laughed at Maybelle laughing.

But something happened that was very upsetting. Kim, the anorexic who eats with Dr. Sandor and comes to the hospital for injections, had a terrible seizure. A severe potassium and thiamine imbalance caused the neurons in her brain to stop firing properly. She lives alone and would have died if her father hadn't just happened to be visiting at the time. She collapsed and went into convulsions, and he had to give her mouth-to-mouth resuscitation. She was still in convulsions when she came into emergency.

The reason that Kim had the seizure is that her weight has gone up and down so many times. She goes down to about eighty-five pounds and then back up to a normal weight, only to go down again. Each time she enters the starvation syndrome, neurons in her brain are damaged. But the brain can't regenerate. Once the damage has been done, it will not heal. Therefore, her "seizure threshold" has been lowered, and she is more and more likely to have seizures.

SUNDAY, MAY 1   Well, my suffering has finally paid off. My weight jumped from 33 to 33.9 kg—almost a whole kilogram, or about 2 pounds. Now I weigh 74.74 pounds. But the best part is that I'm totally happy about it. I'm not scared or upset in the slightest, and I was even able to eat my whole breakfast. Unfortunately, I had my pills too close together last night and I'm pretty hung over now. I'm shaking all over and my body jumps from time to time. I'm also quite dizzy.

Diane says I'll probably be on the Anafranil for about six months after leaving the hospital. It works by blocking a certain part of the brain and lowering the anxiety I sometimes feel when confronted with food. I don't like the idea, but the Anafranil does seem to be helping me. I just wish I had the strength to do it on my own.

Mom and I went out for supper today. I was kind of anxious, but my heart wasn't thumping like it used to. I did very well. I even had milk (one of my old taboos).

Today was the first day in two and a half years that I've experienced hunger. I ate a huge breakfast and was hungry before lunch. I guess my body needs all the extra nourishment. It was a funny feeling, but I'm glad I felt it.

MONDAY, MAY 2   Today I reached 34.2 kg—that's 75.4 pounds! I'm one-third of the way to my goal. Last night I had to shovel a ton of food in at the last minute because my calories weren't high enough. It's so hard to get in twenty-five hundred calories.

I really had to force myself to keep on eating this morning. Usually I gain a few pounds and then feel that I can or must relax the effort for a while. But I'm not going to do that anymore. I gave myself a

75

stern talking to. I can't say that I'm not scared, but at least I don't have that terrible, horrible remorse. All I have to do is remember how miserable I was this weekend, and I keep eating.

I feel pretty optimistic about my weight but very pessimistic about school. I can't study properly while I'm on these pills, and this plan of sending schoolwork back and forth isn't very efficient. It's going to be hard to swallow my pride and accept a few B's.

Kim is conscious now, although her heart has to be monitored since she's already had a cardiac arrest. She refuses to admit that anorexia nervosa caused her problem. She thinks there must be something else wrong with her. She's nuts! These girls (me included) get so carried away. For example, Dr. Sandor told our therapy group this story: He was treating a young girl for anorexia and she was improving. She was almost to her goal weight for her height, which Dr. Sandor said was five foot eight. One day, Dr. Sandor was in his office with a patient when he heard a terrible banging on his door. Then the door burst open and a hysterical, screaming girl fell into the room. She started cursing and swearing at Dr. Sandor, calling him every dirty name in the book. She said (between cusses), "You lied to me to make me fat! You said I was five foot eight and now I find I'm only five foot seven. You made me fat!"

The secretary then came in to try and quiet her down, and the girl started hitting and kicking her. Dr. Sandor hurried over and said, "Please don't hit her." The girl picked up a chair and charged him. Then she threw one of those huge metal ashtrays across the room and ran out of the building screaming and swearing all the way.

Well, Vanessa was finally admitted today. She's so beautiful. She and Rob, the new guy, hit it off right away. I thought they might. I found out that Rob is schizophrenic. He's just here having his medication changed and he seems perfectly normal. He and Vanessa were playing crib till all hours last night. But Vanessa is nuts. "I want to see bones! I love bones!" she says.

I hope it will turn out OK when we room together. She has tons of calorie books and does two hours of calisthenics every morning. She gave up school to pursue a full-time anorexia-bulimia career. I think she says a lot of things just to shock people. So I just don't act surprised. She is a little too thin, but she has a fantastic figure. But what a mixed-up, unhappy girl. I feel so sorry for her. Her parents don't get along and she has "perfect" younger twin brothers. She used to be chubby and her parents were ashamed of her (or she thought they were). So she deliberately set out to become anorexic. She dropped to a normal weight and her parents stopped calling her "disgusting" and "fat pig." But she went further. She got so hungry that she started binging. Then she'd vomit and use laxatives. She told me that once she spent $250 in one day on food in different restaurants. It upsets me when she talks about it. I told her to get the calorie books out of my sight. I'm going to be normal!

TUESDAY, MAY 3   I was up another two points today! That's 34.4 kg, or 75.84 pounds. That means I've gained more than 11 pounds since I've been here. I feel OK about it. I'm very happy because with each new pound I put on I can see and feel the old Maureen returning. She has been hidden away for three years. Food is becoming less and less a part of my life, and my old interests are returning. It's exciting.

Mom and I are both starting to feel restless. I think it's almost time for her to go home. I'm scared to think about that, but I know it would be good for me. I need to grow up emotionally as well as physically.

I went to school all morning and had a fairly good day. At least I kept busy. With all this new work from my own school, I have tons to do. It's so frustrating not to be able to write neatly. My whole body is just shaking all over. This morning when I woke up, I had this terrible feeling I had lost weight. I got up and forced myself to drink a whole bunch of water. I also was dying to go to the bathroom, but I thought any extra weight would help. It turned out my weight was OK.

Dr. Sandor came and talked with Vanessa and me in my room. I told him I wanted my dosage of Anafranil lowered. He said no, he'd given me plenty of opportunity to gain on my own, but I couldn't. He said that the reason my anxiety has diminished so much and I've been able to eat lots but not feel guilty is that the Anafranil is working.

That depressed me. So I'm really not getting better. I got quite upset and said that when I'm taken off the drug I'll go right back to being anorexic. But Dr. Sandor said that I'll be taken off gradually and that once my weight is normal I'll stop thinking unhealthy thoughts that make me scared and skinny. I'll forget about my laws and maybe stop hating myself. I guess I looked kind of sad because he put me on his knee and gave me a kiss. As I was leaving he said, "You are still too skinny, my dear. There's nothing to you."

The group therapy went pretty well. Vanessa and I walked over together. Since she's on level four, she can escort me. That's hardly fair. Her attitude is much worse than mine, and I'm still on level three. Vanessa *wants* to be anorexic. She's extremely proud that she's anorexic and plans to get far worse.

She and Rob are having a ball. They go to Queen Elizabeth Park together and even stay out until after eight o'clock. But Vanessa is nice. She's my friend. Dr. Sandor said she won't be a bad influence on me—I need to "toughen up."

Anyway, the group was good. Two new girls were there. One is eighteen, almost nineteen, and engaged. She is five foot ten and about one hundred pounds. I mean, it's absolutely gross. It made me sick to look at her. Now I know how Mom and Dad must feel. When I walked into the room and saw her, I felt sick and disgusted. I thought, I want absolutely nothing to do with this insane and selfish disease. I don't even want my name to be associated with it. This girl had the "anorexic look"—not just skinniness but a certain pallor that all anorexics have. All anorexics have that funny, ugly hair too—dull, brittle, coarse, and kind of copper colored. Yuck!

She sat there looking like a skeleton and saying she can still "pinch an inch." Her boyfriend told her to lose weight because she was so much taller than he. He thought if she lost enough weight she'd get shorter too. I guess when she hit eighty pounds he was still telling her she was fat. She's been in and out of hospital and reached her goal weight four times, but she always goes back to being anorexic. That's not going to happen to me.

WEDNESDAY, MAY 4   Dr. Sandor came in to see Vanessa and me this morning. Vanessa was still in bed. I had a really good discussion with him and asked him something I've been wondering about for a long time now. He was saying that most anorexics are meticulous and perfectionistic and pay close attention to detail. I asked him if that meant I had to lower my standards. He said no, there's nothing wrong with always striving to do the very best you are capable of in everything. But when it comes to your body, you must be able to recognize your limitations.

78

Dr. Sandor told me that I'm a good judge of character and that I'd make a good psychologist. I'm going to leave here with a fat head as well as a fat body!

I went to school all morning and had a pretty good day, although the teacher's attempts at humor are getting boring. "Now do your work," she says, "or I'll give you twenty lashes with a wet noodle. Hee, hee!"

Rob showed up late, as usual, and told the teacher he wouldn't be able to make it in the afternoon because he had to see his nurse. I could tell he was lying. He and Vanessa took off on a three-hour pass right after lunch.

When I came back at 11:30, Vanessa, Rob, and I sat on Vanessa's bed and listened to her Walkman until the trays came. Vanessa proudly told us that she consumed only two hundred calories yesterday. She's having a ball. If everyone wouldn't give her so much attention when she doesn't eat, it might help.

I had breakfast in the lounge this morning and Martha sat beside me. In the middle of the meal, she suddenly grabbed her box of Medi-wipes, clutched it to her breast, and said, "I was just getting it through to that fellow that I must have my Medi-wipes to identify myself!" She then went on to praise me for my great courage in identifying myself.

THURSDAY, MAY 5 Well, today was moving day. We are finally back on the original C-1. I packed up all my junk last night so I'd be ready and could go to school for an hour or so. I had one suitcase, three big black garbage bags, a huge duffel bag, and a purse. We loaded it all onto a cart and I struggled along behind with my arms full of school books, plants, and various other paraphernalia.

The ward is all fixed up. Now it's the nicest ward in all of Shaughnessy. It's on the basement level, just past the cafeteria. The walls are covered with beige, sort of tweed-looking wallpaper, and the carpet is a brown twist. At one end, there's a huge dining room with little round tables and comfortable chairs. Past that is a lounge with big easy chairs, a stereo, a piano, and crib boards. At the other end of the hall, there's a lounge with a TV set, pool tables, a ping-pong table, and comfortable couches. There's also an exercise bike (that pleases Vanessa). I have a room with Vanessa and April, although there are also single, double, and four-bed bedrooms. The bedrooms have long, skinny bulletin boards on the walls, wooden closets, and finished bedside tables that match the headboards—and don't squeak.

Some friends from Cranbrook happened to be in town today, so they came to see me. After they left, April's nurse told me I can't have visitors in the room because it upsets April too much. Mom and I can't even play cards here.

April is getting worse. She slit her wrists yesterday, but her primary nurse caught her and quickly got a doctor to stitch them up. April showed me the huge, mean red cuts on both arms. It made me upset. Maybe that's what she wants.

I said, "Were you trying to kill yourself or just hurt yourself?"

She said she only wanted to injure herself because she feels guilty for other people's problems. She thinks it's her fault that her sister's baby died of sudden infant death syndrome. She blames herself because her fifteen-year-old daughter got pregnant and ended up having an abortion. She thinks her son hates her. She doesn't like herself, and she just can't break out of that dark little world of self-pity. Her mother is mad at her and writes letters saying, "You should be home with your children!"

April doesn't say much, and then out of the blue she'll suddenly tell you some big personal problem she has. I guess one must keep in mind that she is crazy. It's hard to put that delicately. What is the definition of "crazy"?

Vanessa is doing a little better today. She needs a lot of encouragement, prodding, and praise—not to mention constant watching so that she doesn't vomit. All she ate yesterday was four grains of rice and a lettuce leaf. I'm doing all the things with her that Mom does for me, including eating more myself. Vanessa says I'm really helping her. I hope so—I'd hate to see her get as awful looking as I was. At least she's not sixty-four pounds. She's too thin, but she manages to look pretty good. I feel an obligation to help her in any way I can because of all the support I get from family and friends. And although I think she's a bit phony, I really like Vanessa. I'm learning how to be a teenager with her.

Right now Vanessa figures it's sweet and true love with her and Rob. He's going home tomorrow, so they went for a long walk at Queen Elizabeth Park until after ten o'clock. She came back with red eyes. "I just cried buckets! And would you look at my hair? Why, I look ghastly!"

Dr. Sandor said I could be on level four, but I said no, I don't deserve it yet. I had probably my best day ever because I ate without guilt. Two of my biggest fears are greatly diminished—butter and drinks like milk and juice. Today I used my whole pat of butter, drank a cup of milk, and even had juice with Caloreen. I've learned to use these things because they are a good way to get the calories without actually eating and chewing. "You're learning," Diane says. Most anorexics eat greater amounts of low-calorie foods instead of having a few higher-calorie foods to make up the same caloric intake for the day. But I hate feeling so full. Butter and liquids just kind of slide down and don't fill you up.

MONDAY, MAY 9   I had a super weekend, but I feel pretty low today because my weight went down almost 0.6 kg, or about a pound.

We went shopping on Saturday, and I bought some new clothes to fit my new body. I still look horrible in pants, but it's coming.

On Sunday night when I came back to the hospital, I felt sad. Vanessa and Samantha were depressed too. We sat at the kitchen table and talked it out. They had both binged severely all weekend. For Vanessa, eating just a little teeny bit more than she is supposed to will trigger a binge. She ate all her meal, all of my meal (it came even though I wasn't there), my leftover muffin, leftover food from other trays, and two loaves of white bread from the kitchen. Then she vomited it all up.

Samantha is pretty discouraged because she's been here for two months and hasn't lost a pound. And she still binges every day. I asked Vanessa how she felt when she was binging, and she said she feels nothing—not guilt or disgust or enjoyment. It doesn't matter what the food is, or how moldy or dirty it is, she'll eat it. One day she ate a loose-leaf paper out of her binder. She even ate Edna's slobbery leftovers. Then she went into the bathroom and silently threw it up just two feet away from someone.

I said, "How can you stand to look down a toilet?"

She said, "It's the most common scene in my life."

I wish there were something, anything, I could do for Samantha and Vanessa. But I guess I better just worry about myself. Diane says I don't get a pass next weekend because I lost weight over this weekend. I'll get that weight back, though.

Last night April stayed over another night at home, so Vanessa and I had the room to ourselves. We talked until midnight and she told me a few things that almost curled my hair. She used to be a chubby little teacher's pet. One day everybody turned against her and threw snowballs at her, calling her "fat pig" and "apple polisher." She decided to change, and change she did. She lost fifty pounds, started smoking pot, took acid, sniffed cocaine, and lost her virginity at age twelve. She was terrified when that happened. Poor Vanessa — she's much older than her age. She finds my naiveté hilarious. I think it's a pathetic consequence of anorexia nervosa. I'm never out with the gang learning the facts of life.

I knew I couldn't escape the wrath of the mighty Chris, the witch nurse. She came back from Hawaii today with her brown skin, blunt, thin hair, and false eyelashes. "Look, Maureen," she said after school, "if I have it my way, you won't be going to school at all." I walked away. I had no idea why she was mad, so I assumed it was because I lost weight.

Dad phoned me at the pay phone, and when I told him what Chris had said he said, "You tell Chris I said that's ridiculous, and if she wants to dispute that, she can call me." Good old dad — he's a "real man."

I discovered something interesting on the weekend. I found that there are certain words that are very difficult for me to say. When it is necessary to say such words as "cream," "fat," and "hair" in ordinary conversation, I have to force them out. Cream is a fattening thing. It is so forbidden to me that the word is almost like a swearword. It is vulgar and horrible. I cannot say the word "hair" without thinking of my own lack thereof. My hair used to be my best feature. Now it's my worst — and that doesn't leave much. I'm so conscious of hair. Some people have asked me why I am always touching my head. It's because I have to assure myself that there is indeed some hair left, that it hasn't all fallen out within the last few minutes.

TUESDAY, MAY 10   Today I'm right back up to where I was before I lost weight (75.9 pounds). I got brave last night and ate a chocolate bar with my milk. I didn't think I could do it, but I did. I'm finding I *can*, physically, eat anything. It's not impossible, but it sure is hard. I'm proud of myself.

Chris doesn't seem to share my enthusiasm, however. She apparently told Dr. Sandor that I have gained only two pounds since I came in. That's why she threatened to take me out of school. Diane says I should ask her why she said that. I'm nervous, but Diane seems to think I should be more assertive. Dr. Sandor says I'm tough—"little but strong." I wonder. He said that if I can gain another kilogram, or about two pounds, this week I'll get my weekend pass. I'll keep trying.

WEDNESDAY, MAY 11   The sky is so blue and clear! I feel good, really good, because it's spring and I'm recovering from a three-year nightmare. I went outside to the garden just off the kitchen and sat on a blanket in the sun. I wanted to savor every little bit of it. I can start living again. I never realized how depressed I was. When a person's life is dominated by food, there is nothing else. An abstainer's life revolves around food. The school's Spring Fair is canceled, but that's okay—I get a chicken wing for lunch. I can't go to the dance, because I might get behind in my schoolwork. But it doesn't matter—I get a peach half for dessert. And on and on it goes, until everything is gone. It's all empty except for the stringent diet plan. That's all an abstainer has. It's the one thing she can control. All the former interests, plans, hobbies, enthusiasm, and fun are gone. No wonder everything looked dark to me—I was living in an unreal, selfish world.

I can see that even now I am far too emotional about food. I plan what I'm going to eat days in advance, and my whole schedule revolves around mealtimes. But I used to live in fear that we would be invited out for dinner or that Dad would offer to take the family to a restaurant for lunch. I would eat very little all day so that just in case we went out I wouldn't be terrified of going over my caloric limit for the day. Some days I limited myself to five hundred calories; other days it was eight hundred, one thousand, and sometimes up to fourteen hundred.

But often we didn't go out and I would have had very few calories that day. Instead of eating up to my limit, I would just leave it at that. I can remember going to bed one night so exhausted from studying all day and not eating enough that I felt as if I were going to die. I suspected then that this behavior couldn't go on forever. Something had to give. I was so jumpy all the time and cried at the slightest provocation.

I talk as if I'm completely recovered now; yet I'm not even halfway.

But if I feel this much better at seventy-six pounds, I'll feel fantastic at eighty-five or ninety (I hope). But my fears linger still. I don't want to be fat or self-indulgent or lazy.

I'm learning how to relax a little, though. Last night, for the first time in years, I spent the evening doing something I enjoy. Instead of studying or reading classic literature, I just sat on the bed and talked with Vanessa. She told me all about her life, and, by the time she had finished, I could see why she became bulimic. Her story makes me appreciate my family and leaves me wondering why I developed a similar affliction.

"My parents are high-class snobs," she said. "Appearances are so important to them." Her parents are both English, and Vanessa herself was born in Bristol. They own a magnificent house on beach-front property. Vanessa gets a car at graduation. She was her parents' pride and joy, an absolute whiz at school. But there was one serious problem that marred the family name. Vanessa was a chub. Fat is not socially acceptable. She was ridiculed at home. Her brothers called her "fat pig," and her parents bugged her incessantly. In grade six her mother told Vanessa she couldn't go to the fair that was in town because she was "an embarrassment to the family." All she would do was "eat, eat, eat!" Vanessa set out to become anorexic, following the examples provided in countless glossy magazine articles about Cherry Boone, Karen Carpenter, Jane Fonda, and others. Vanessa started to lose weight, but her parents insisted she eat meals with them. Her solution was simple. She started practicing the art of vomiting into chip bags. Around this time she also got heavily involved in alcohol, drugs, and sex.

One day her body couldn't take any more dieting, and she binged. That set the precedent for the next two years. Her life was diet, binge, vomit, diet, binge, vomit. The very word "binge" upsets me. I can't stand to write down some of the details of these binges because it's too awful.

She said her parents fight constantly. I asked her if they love each other. "No, definitely not," she said, without hesitating. Her father buys all the porn magazines, and she's known about it for years. She sounded so bitter, so toughened by life. It made me sad to hear her talk so blatantly about the problems in her family.

We cried together for a while and then laughed because we are so different. She's done it all, and I've run away from it all. Neither

84

one of us is right. Last night I wished I could take away all the things that hurt Vanessa. She's just a little girl; yet she's also a toughened, middle-aged woman.

We had a pretty good group therapy session yesterday. It was packed. About ten of us were all squeezed into Dr. Sandor's office. Tiffany, the mother anorexic, is trying at last and has started to make minimal progress. Another girl gained five pounds and feels so much better. Yesterday she began to menstruate again. I was so happy for her, I could have cried. I wanted to give her a hug, but I thought the other girls might roll their eyes.

Kim is still being kept in the hospital, but she came to the group too. It was terrible. Her head was like a skull on the top of a toothpick. She looked dead. Her eyes were sunken and ringed with black. I could still see a little hole in her hand from the i.v. She talked quite a bit and told us all that we were selfish and that anorexia nervosa was nothing to be proud of. Most of us agreed.

Kim is very masochistic. She feels she must discipline herself. At university she burned herself several times and kept bumping into things. When I really think about it, I can see some masochistic tendencies in myself. Just the other day I found myself deliberately putting my hands on the heater until they were burnt. I don't know why. I just wanted to see how long I could stand to keep them there. I never consciously decided to hurt myself.

Yesterday and this morning the four eating-disorder patients on C-1 had a conference with Dr. Sandor. I put my arm around Chris and apologized for the misunderstanding. I don't know why I did that since it was she who accused me of gaining two pounds when I've actually gained twelve. She said that I should have asked her why she said that and got the situation straightened out. Instead I spoke to Diane. That made Chris really mad. She said she was mad at me for "sulking" too. I was unaware of committing such an atrocity. Oh well, Dr. Sandor likes me. He says I'm a nice little girl but that I've got to become a nice big girl, physically and emotionally. Everyone wants Mom to go home. I think I'm ready for that too.

Life has calmed down since we moved down to the new ward. For one thing, there are no old men groaning or pooping on the floor. I keep things kind of exciting, though. Last night I had a pretty heavy collective-bargaining session with John, the male nurse. I wanted to go over to King Edward Mall with Mom. He said I'd have to have a chocolate bar because if I lost weight Diane would break his neck. I said no way, but would he possibly settle for a chocolate-chip cookie? "Nope," he said. We argued for about five minutes while Mom stood there in shocked silence. Finally I drew the line. "Two cookies—that's my final offer. Take it or leave it." He took it and I left.

My weight was up another 0.3 kg today, or 0.66 pound, and no one can imagine the feeling I had when I put on a skirt that didn't fall down on my hips. I was very pleased and proud. I ran to the mirror, but I still saw that pale, drawn anorexic face. It's never looked so ugly to me.

At lunch time, I ate two—yes, two—pieces of chicken, and one of them had skin on it. I also drank my milk and ate my bread and fruit. I felt OK when I did it, but later that old panic set in. I tried to just put it out of my mind, but guilt kept nagging at me. My stomach looked bigger every minute. Sometimes, even with the Anafranil, it's really hard.

Vanessa and I both remember too clearly our first days on the psych ward. Most of my bad attitudes and fears about people on the ward have been dispelled. There are no murderers or rapists. No one is violent or throws things around. The other day as I was opening the door I looked at the sign that says,"All visitors report to the nurses' station" and thought about how I used to have such contempt for and prejudice against people on any psychiatric ward. And here I was calmly walking in there as if it were my home. All the people who have come and gone on this ward have been outstandingly nice. I will never forget Vanessa and Samantha or Joe or Martha (who hugs me and says what a brave little girl I am for identifying myself). I think life is harder on nice people.

FRIDAY, MAY 13 I had to gain four whole points of a kilogram, which is almost a pound. And I had to gain it overnight. I almost made it—almost. I woke up at 6:00 A.M., dying of apprehension and suspense. The nurse weighed me because I was shaking much too hard to do it myself. I needed to be 35.4 kg (78 pounds), and I couldn't believe it when the scale came to rest on exactly 35.3 (77.82 pounds). "Maybe he'll let me go anyway," I said hopefully.

The nurse looked doubtful but sympathetic. "Ask him," she said.

I didn't go to school because I wanted to wait around until

86

Dr. Sandor came. Chris said he was going to be on the radio at 9:00, but I couldn't find the station. I worked on my algebra and got extremely frustrated with functions in point-slope form. Vanessa ended up helping me.

At 10:30 Dr. Sandor and Chris came into my room. I told Dr. Sandor that I was a single point away from my required weight for the week and asked him if I could go away for the weekend anyway.

He put a fatherly arm around me and kissed me on the forehead. "I like you," he said. "You're a sweet girl. Yes, you can go, dear."

I thanked him profusely, but Chris immediately said, "The head nurse and I want to talk to you about that." That made me nervous. The sky was so blue, and it was so hot and sunny. I wanted that pass very badly.

After they left, I went down the hall to the pay phone so that I could let Mom know I'd be out at 4:00. The phone is just around the corner from the head nurse's office. Sheena is the head nurse on C-1. She looks like a model and talks like a dictator. If there's one thing that woman is not short of, it's pride. I was about to make my phone call, when I heard terrible shrieks coming from her office.

"That's not the point!" Sheena bellowed. "We work hard all week to help these girls, to remold their thinking, their attitudes, and you waltz in here and ruin it all!"

"It's only one point of a kilogram," Dr. Sandor said meekly.

"I don't care," she screamed. "This girl is not making enough progress. She shouldn't be allowed out!"

Dr. Sandor persisted. So did Sheena. "I completely withdraw my support and the rest of the staff's support from this case."

I couldn't believe my ears. I walked around the corner and said, "If it's going to cause that much of a problem, I'll stay."

But Dr. Sandor said no. He said, "I want you to go out and have fun, but please, for God's sake *eat!*"

When I phoned Mom to tell her, I said, "Mom, we've really got to try hard this weekend." She said, "No, *you've* got to try hard."

To make sure I would start the weekend off right, I ate some ice cream. It was difficult and made me feel sick, but I ate it because I knew I had to. Somehow that took most of the guilt away. After that we hopped on a bus and went downtown. We met Auntie Peg later for supper. I felt a bit apprehensive because I felt a little nauseated. But I knew everything would be all right. I'd eaten in this particular restaurant before and lived. Besides, I was still full of enthusiasm for my high-calorie weekend. I ordered trout. It came with corn and a dinner roll. I thought I would be fine. But when it was put in front of me, the plate looked so full! The fish smelled fishy, and my stomach turned over. My heart began to pound and my eyes filled with tears. I couldn't touch it. I couldn't even bear to eat the corn or the dinner roll. I didn't want to touch the tea. I felt greasy and grimy all over, and I couldn't stand to sit there with it in front of me. I went to the ladies' room and cried like a little baby. I was disgusted and very disappointed in myself. There was that perfectly good food out there getting cold. And I had thought I was almost cured! I felt so discouraged. I paid for my own dinner because I felt so guilty. But I just couldn't wait to get out of that restaurant and away from those smells and all the dirty dishes on people's tables. I continued to feel sick all evening. I ended up eating supper at Auntie Peg's around midnight. What an idiot!

SUNDAY NIGHT, MAY 15   The weekend was great! After Friday night, I ate very well and with very little fear. It sure feels funny to pinch a little bit of flesh around my stomach. The new weight is hard to adjust to.

MONDAY, MAY 16   I feel horrible. My weight fell two points over the weekend. And I tried so hard.

Vanessa was crying for me this morning. Actually she was crying for herself too, and Samantha. Sheena really did it this time. Right in front of us she threw a temper tantrum. She screamed, "I don't give a damn about any of them anymore. As far as I'm concerned, they can starve, binge, or puke as much as they want. I don't care. They're just a bunch of bitches!" I was too shocked to defend myself, but Vanessa, tears streaming down her face, said, "This little thing ate m & m's, a whole bag of chips, which she hates, a muffin, and a cup of whole milk! Don't you dare say she isn't trying!"

Her voice was shaking and her tirade was scattered with curses and assorted obscenities. She was pretty upset herself because she gained three pounds overnight. She had at last eaten normally while out on a pass with her mother. She was very happy last night.

This morning she said she didn't want to be weighed because it would upset her, but the nurse insisted. Vanessa panicked and binged. I should have been watching her, but because I don't understand bulimia, it never crossed my mind. I tried to talk soothingly and calm her down while she sat with her eyes closed, biting her hands and scratching her arms. Her behavior scared me.

Tonight I ate a chocolate bar. It took me quite a long time, but I ate it. I felt pretty good about it too.

Well, I was sure kept busy all day. After breakfast, I worked on math. Then I went to school and studied until 10:40. Then I came back to the ward and met Mom, and we went to Dr. Sandor's lecture from 11:00 to 1:00. It was OK, even though I'd heard most of it before.

After the lecture, I had lunch, which I ate ravenously. And it only took about forty minutes. When I first came here, it took an hour. Then I studied until 3:30 and went to my group therapy meeting at the pavilion. More studying when I got back, supper, visiting, more studying.

Samantha is being discharged on Friday. She looks the same as she did when she came in and is still binging, but she seems happy and satisfied with the results of her treatment. I'll miss her very much. I need Samantha to keep telling me I look good. This new weight makes me feel hot and sluggish. Sometimes my legs look huge to me. But I tell myself that's ridiculous. I'm learning to squash those destructive thoughts.

I've been running into a bit of trouble with Vanessa. She's been binging for the last three days. My m & m's and my chocolate cookies are missing from my drawer. My snacks, or bits of them, have mysteriously disappeared. It makes me angry, but I don't want to hurt Vanessa's feelings. She keeps asking, "Are you peeved with me?" And I say no. I am annoyed, but she can't help herself. It's just the invasion of privacy I mind.

At 8:00 we had a ward meeting. All the patients acted like a bunch of children, complaining that they shouldn't have to empty the laundry hampers and squabbling over how late the kitchen should be open or the TV left on. It was ridiculous and disgusting.

Ian phoned just after the meeting. I think he had been drinking because he didn't make much sense.

89

Many people who starved during the war became bulimic. Conditions of starvation:
— loss of menstruation
— irritability
— difficulty in staying warm
— inability to concentrate
— fatigue, listlessness
— lowered metabolism

Anorexia nervosa has reached epidemic proportions, increasing by a factor of three in the last ten years.

One hundred years ago, there were no jeans, and a large bust and bum were in style.

Women wore stays and corsets to achieve this look; one girl died when her ribs grew into her liver.

Miss America has only 80 percent of normal weight. Twenty years ago she had 91 percent.

Tubular figure in style — if this tendency continues, either children won't be conceived or they will be born with brain damage.

Models in *Vogue* magazine show anorexic lines on their faces.

Ten percent of female doctors are anorexics.

Lack of hormones is a result, not a cause of anorexia nervosa.

No diets work! Only exercise works.

You can't manipulate your body into being something it isn't without feeling the consequences.

Diet centers don't tell you that you must lose slowly. Many people who go start binging.

In bulimics, the stomach won't release the hormones that tell you you're full — these hormones were destroyed by starvation.

Some bulimic patients drink the hormones in liquid form to suppress the appetite.

Depression causes regression, and patients become more dependent on family members.

TUESDAY, MAY 17   This morning I was up at 6:30 and waiting by the pay phone by 7:00. That's 8:00 Cranbrook time, which is when my teachers were phoning. They all gave me encouragement and assigned lots of work. The next two weeks I'm going to do nothing but study. I'll pass those exams or die trying. But somehow my attitude toward school is a little different now. I think I'm getting a little calmer and a little more reasonable. All my goals were just too far out of reach. I was striving for perfection — "striving after wind."

WEDNESDAY, MAY 18   Everybody on this ward smokes — I mean *everybody*. It's odd and quite disgusting the way each person has his or her own characteristic smoking style. Vanessa inhales deeply and releases the smoke through her nose. She looks like a dragon exhaling fire. Sometimes she opens one corner of her mouth and lets the smoke seep out that way. She can also form teeny little rings of smoke. Now that's talent!

April looks grotesquely ugly when she's smoking. She puckers up her mouth and caves in her cheeks to inhale. Then she licks her lips in the most repulsive way and slowly exhales.

But Dean, an older man on the ward, really takes the cake. You can hear him coming from miles away because he exhales with a thunderous "Th Thhhhhhhe." I watch him inhale, count to two, and say to myself, "I know, I know — Th Thhhhhhhe." It is so loud and so continuous that sometimes I want to scream. Thank heavens he's leaving today.

Martha is a really nice person, but she's slightly odd too. Just when I think she's OK, she says or does something weird again. Just before she was admitted, the family went out for dinner and left Martha at home alone for the evening, since she didn't want to go out. When they returned, they found her busily painting the fridge bright red.

Veronica is worse. She has no teeth and is quite disgusting. She always forgets to fill out her menu and then asks in a demanding voice, "Did everybody get liver tonight?" The other day at breakfast, she picked up her French toast, ripped it in half, folded each half twice, and ate it with her fingers while the syrup slowly dripped out. Then at lunch she decided she really didn't care for her food. So while Edna was away moaning "Oh goodness me, oh dear" in the nurses' station, Veronica snitched her chocolate pudding. Edna returned, ate a little off her tray, and put it back on the cart. She disappeared for a moment, moaning and complaining, and then returned. Again she ate a little off her tray and put it back on the cart. She repeated this procedure eight or ten times until the nurses finally medicated her and she zonked out in her room.

Old Alice is another beauty. She loves to sit on her bed or in the lounge and pick her nose. Then she acts confused and annoyed when she gets a nosebleed. But what I really like is when these ladies stand over me with their teeth out and their hands on their hips and say, "That looks like a lovely meal, dear. You eat it now, that's a good girl." They're especially bad when they've just had shock treatments. It makes them pretty foggy.

FRIDAY, MAY 20   Poor Vanessa! She is on six-hour bed rest—two hours after every meal. She can't even go to the bathroom. Nor can she sit up and do exercises. She's pretty mad. "Dr. Sandor's a creep," a large sign above her bed proclaims. April eventually took it down.

Life is pretty tough for Vanessa right now. More and more comes out as we talk and get to know each other better. She tried to kill her mom once. She went into a rage and ran after her with a knife. Her mother ran and locked herself in the bathroom. Vanessa's been picked up for shoplifting three times. The second and third times she was stealing food to satisfy one of her urges to binge. I asked Vanessa what her parents did when she was arrested. "After the third time, they gave me dirty looks. Three days later we left for England," she said. She's done sixty hours of community work to pay for her sins. Poor, poor, little Vanessa. How can this girl—this little girl, really—with the soft brown curls be full of so much bad? Underneath, she is probably just the same as me. Although she seems the opposite, I think Vanessa is insecure.

The bed rest is a punishment for the terrible binges she's had in the last few days. She showed me the wrappers in her garbage can. The work of a single hour: two cheesecakes, three bags of cookies, a huge bag of m & m's, licorice all-sorts, two bags of chips, several chocolate bars, a hamburger, and onion rings. When I left her alone for just an hour while I went to school, she went down to King Edward Mall and reduced the forty dollars her mother left her to four dollars. Then she vomited everything up. Vanessa told me she spent most of her time in the park washroom alternately stuffing chips into her mouth and barfing. It upset me to hear all this, and I asked her to stop.

I got some good news yesterday. I am 79.65 pounds, so in con-

92

ference yesterday with all the nurses and Dr. Sandor I asked to go on level four. They said yes! I also get to go to the cafeteria now. I got a food card so that I can get my meals free. However, they've decided that if I don't gain exactly one kilogram (2.2 pounds) every week, according to a weigh-in on Friday, I get no passes, no visitors, no school, no cafeteria card, and no trips to the library upstairs. One fatso nurse suggested to Dr. Sandor that I have a time limit on my meals and that I shouldn't be allowed to read while I eat. I got quite mad, and Dr. Sandor said those restrictions were unnecessary.

Today I just studied and did homework all day. I hate studying now, but Mom said, "Good. That's more normal." It sure feels funny to actually fill my clothes again. But I like it. I like having a body.

I went down to the cafeteria for supper at 5:30. I panicked and turned away just before the woman served my sweet-and-sour pork. But a few minutes later I went back and got some. It was OK! While I was eating it, I couldn't help but think that just a month ago that giant plateful of food all close together would have been totally impossible for me to eat. All day I've had this funny feeling, like someone is missing. It feels like a family member is gone. I think it's me. I've changed so much in the last two months that I feel like a new person. Sometimes I miss the old me, but not very often.

I felt nauseated and a little bit depressed all night. It's all this schoolwork mixed with the fact that Mom is leaving for good on Sunday, I guess.

I was sitting outside in the sun around 3:30 when a woman and a severely anorexic girl came to talk to me. They're from Edmonton, and the girl, Tammy, is being admitted to the general ward on Tuesday. Her face is angular and pale. She looks horrid. It turns out that she is fifteen and a bulimic-anorexic. Poor kid—I'm glad I don't look like that anymore. I was disgusted to hear Vanessa and Tammy competing to see who was sicker. Vanessa gave a detailed description of her last binge and proudly announced that she has lanugo on her stomach. "I used to be anorexic," she kept saying. Even I fell into it a little. "You should have seen me two months ago!" I said.

Vanessa lives and breathes food. I told her my little cousin was in the hospital. "What did he have for dinner?" Vanessa asked. Every time I come back from the cafeteria she asks me what I had, and I must describe the meal in minute detail.

She knows every little bit of food I have in the room. She told me that she even went through my purse and knew I was keeping some peanuts there for emergencies. "I just like to know it's there," she said. "I need to look at it."

SUNDAY, MAY 22　This morning I jumped out of bed at 6:30, had a shower, ate breakfast, and was busily studying by 8:00. While I was in the cafeteria, Martha came to sit with me. It was terrible. She kept telling me the same story over and over again. And, to make matters worse, it was the same silly story she told me last night at dinner. "I was so intent on getting here I forgot. . . . I see they cut you half a grapefruit. I wonder why they put yours in a . . . My companions and I are on a salt-free diet and is it Sunday today?"

I bashed my brains out over algebra all morning just like I've done for the last month. I got more and more scared and upset and felt very panicky, or "anxious," as they say around here. Finally, in a state of near-hysteria, tears coursing down my cheeks, I realized that Algebra II isn't worth a nervous breakdown. I'll have to just give up and try to pick it up next year.

Mom's plane left this morning. I miss her already, but things will be OK. Diane says I've grown up a great deal in the last two months.

Vanessa and I went for a little walk. The weather was gorgeous, so she wore shorts, a tube top, and high-heeled thongs. Some guys in a convertible honked and waved at her. She did look pretty nice. But as we walked past all the shops in King Edward Mall, she looked at her reflection constantly in the windows. I don't think she hates her body quite as much as she lets on. She isn't ashamed to undress in front of me, anyway.

Vanessa and I were talking last night because April is off on a pass. Anyway I discovered that I'm atrociously naive. When she told me that Rob always came in to see her at night, I automatically assumed that he sat on the end of her bed and they had a nice discussion. Ha! I've got a lot to learn.

I studied social studies for the rest of the day. I took a break from 3:00 to 4:30 and sat in the sun. "Come and get some rays," Vanessa said.

Another patient of Dr. Sandor's is on the ward now. She is an odd one—an obsessive. Karen constantly washes—she goes through four bars of soap a day. Every time I go into the bathroom, there she

94

is amid tons and tons of lather. She even wipes the soap clean when she's done with it and cleans the sink. It's really unbelievable. My own desire to wash all the time has lessened a great deal. I don't always feel dirty anymore.

After supper tonight we sat in our room and talked to Diane. She told us a little bit about April and about people's different coping mechanisms. Her psychology professor had told the class two interesting stories on this topic:

A nurse who worked the night shift had to cross a big field in the dark. She did this every day going to and coming from work. One day a nurse got raped near the area. The woman who was crossing the field became nervous and started carrying a rock with her as she went across the field. Then she started carrying two rocks, one in each hand. She reasoned that if one rock was good, two must be better. Eventually she ended up dragging a huge sack full of rocks all the way across the field every day. She was always exhausted at work, but she had a compulsive obsession to carry all these rocks. Of course this arrangement did her absolutely no good. It was simply her coping mechanism.

The other story was about a little boy whose mother worked all day. The boy came home every day for lunch, and, because he was alone, his mother reminded him every morning to make sure the stove was off before he left. The boy was afraid he would forget, and, after getting two blocks away, he would run back to check the stove. Eventually, when his grades began to drop, a psychiatrist found that he was running home between classes to check that the stove was off.

Later on Vanessa asked me to play Trivial Pursuit, but I felt compelled to study, even though I'd already spent hours at it. Vanessa got really mad at me. She said I was being stupid and just had to lighten up and let myself have some fun. It was the best thing she could have done—I saw the light at last. "Why not?" I asked myself. I played Trivial Pursuit and had a great time. I had so much fun and laughed so hard! It felt good to laugh again. I even had the energy for it!

TUESDAY, MAY 24 We had a good therapy session today. Four out of seven people at our sessions are models. One girl who is five foot ten and weighs a hundred pounds was told by her photographer to lose five more pounds. Her parents practically forced a modeling career on her, and she hates it. She hates the attitudes, the competition, and the way the agents go around poking everyone in the stomach. She has a tattoo of a bumblebee on her, shall we say, cleavage.

We discussed the relationship between the tattoo and her anorexia nervosa. She said, "I wanted to shock everyone, to do something my family would never dream of doing. I mean, my sisters just about died when they saw that I actually went out and put a smiling bumblebee on my bosom!" We all cracked up.

I did really well with my eating all day. I ate a big coffee ice cream cone, and I had fries with my hamburger at supper. That's sure a breakthrough. And I don't even like French fries. I just hope all this hard work pays off. I have to gain a pound and half in two days.

Vanessa has been doing very well. This is her seventh day with no binging or vomiting. And she's also quit smoking. I'm proud of her. Her parents have invited Dr. Sandor to come to their town. Actually, they are practically begging him to come and give a lecture on anorexia nervosa and bulimia. There seems to be a real plague of it there. Vanessa said that at least ten people who go to her school are either bulimic or anorexic. Dr. Sandor puts the figures at four thousand in Vancouver alone.

I guess maybe I've been studying just a bit too hard. Vanessa said that about three this morning I was writhing around on the bed screaming, "MacKenzie King! MacKenzie King!" I also frequently wake up crying and shaking all over. Yet I don't remember any bad dreams. It must be a side effect of the Anafranil.

WEDNESDAY, MAY 25 The ward dining room is an interesting place to be during a meal. I eat in the cafeteria now, but I like to go back and sit in the dining room to observe. Alice insists on picking her nose between bites. She talks with her mouth full of mashed potatoes. She recently had some shock treatments, and they made her much worse. The other day I said, "Do you know when you're going home, Alice?"

She looked blank. "I have something wrong with me," she said slowly. "I had another problem, but the shock treatments made me lose my memory. I have it back now though!"

I said, "What was wrong before?"

"It?...uh...humm!"

Ten minutes later I walked past her again, and she suddenly looked enlightened. "Depression!" she squealed. "That's what it was!" I was expecting a complex, twelve-syllable medical term and was disappointed to get this general term instead.

Alice gets all dressed up in a skirt and blazer, takes out her keys, and stands by the door with her purse in hand. She stands there all day because she thinks she's going home. At night she crawls into bed fully clothed and confused because she's still on the ward.

Veronica is an equally odd case. She simply can't get it through her head that the meals are chosen and all are different. She gets roast beef and just figures everyone has roast beef. Yesterday at lunch she said, "This isn't where we ate yesterday. We were in, um...Shaughnessy."

"What's this I'm eating?" she asks.

"It looks like seafood," Vanessa replies. "I have curried chicken."

"How's *your* seafood?" she asks someone else.

Vanessa patiently explains once again that the patients fill out the menus the night before, and all order different things.

Veronica looks blank. She takes another few bites. "How's *your* seafood, Joseph?"

"I don't have seafood," Joseph says. "I have roast pork."

Veronica looks at her plate again. "Well, it sure looks like fish."

Vanessa rolls her eyes, Alice picks her nose, and a new woman, Polly, spills her soup. She's almost convulsing, and odd groans escape between bites of bread.

The other day we were in the middle of a community meeting when Polly stumbled into the room. She stood in the center of the group. "I decided to come!"

"How nice," Diane said quietly. "Now, can we have another volunteer for laundry on...?"

"I'll just try to sit it out!" Polly yells.

"Wonderful," Vanessa says.

Karen, the hand washer, is very nice. She's twenty-six years old and very skinny and pretty. One night we were playing Trivial Pursuit with her, and she told us all about her problem. She uses her own soap now instead of the hospital's and still goes through four bars a day. When she was at her worst, she washed her hands for seven hours after going to the bathroom. And soap wasn't good enough. She went through bottle after bottle of stringent cleanser. Her hands are dry, cracked, and bleeding. Everybody thought that she was here for anorexia nervosa. She does have a definite tendency that way. She thinks she's got a fat stomach even though she's a total bone-rack. Her compulsive hand washing is very similar to the obsessiveness of anorexia nervosa—it overwhelms everything else. Karen says that there are a lot of people out there who have the problem, but no one sees them because they're all in the bathroom washing their hands.

THURSDAY, MAY 26   Yesterday I pigged out as much as I could because I was terrified I wouldn't be able to gain enough weight for the weekend. I ate more than I thought I ever could and gained a whole kilogram, or 2.2 pounds, by today, ensuring my weekend pass. The staff was very pleased with me, and I went happily off to school. I was still feeling a bit tense about exams, though.

After I had been studying about an hour, the teacher came in. She said, "I was just talking to your school." I immediately felt on guard. She went on to say, in her accusing manner, that the school said I could write my exams in September or October. She then accused me of lying to her and keeping my work secretive. I tried to stay calm. I said, "I told you that they said I could write them later, and you suggested I write them now." My voice was shaking.

The teacher grew red in the face. "I said no such thing!" I knew I was going to cry. "Just sit down and act your age!" she said. "You will stay here and finish your algebra."

All I could think was that she had screwed up all my carefully planned arrangements. I had made a big decision, and I had done it on my own. I had learned to live with it, and now she was dragging it all up again. I kept remembering what Vanessa had said: "Get mad! Quit being such a coward! Stick up for your rights!" I started putting my books back in my school bag. "I don't want to talk about it, and don't you dare say I'm not acting my age!" I started to leave; I wasn't going to let her see me cry. She started after me, so I ran. She ran too.

"Maureen!" she screeched.

"What?" I said, still running.

"What's your local?"

"I have no idea!"

"Yes, you do," she said.

I yelled, "I do not!" and ran onto the elevator. I walked back to the ward and burst into tears on Vanessa's shoulder. My nurse for the day, a "float," came in, and I told her what happened. After that, I started to calm down. I couldn't believe I had asserted myself for the first time. I didn't feel bad about it, but I didn't feel particularly good either.

"I'm never going back to that stupid school," I said.

So after lunch Vanessa and I walked to Queen Elizabeth Park. We put our feet in the little stream and talked. Then we climbed to the top of the hill and went to the conservatory. We were dying of thirst because the day was so hot and we had walked a long way. We went into a grubby little café, and a little Chinese lady charged each of us fifteen cents for about half a cup of water in a paper cup. After that, we went down to a beautiful little garden valley in the park and sat by a waterfall. We talked for about an hour—about abortion, of all things. Underneath that tough exterior, I think Vanessa is very sensitive and caring.

We didn't get back until just about suppertime because we stopped at Big Scoop for a coffee brickle cone. Mmmmm—I ate almost the whole thing. We had a good afternoon, and I didn't even feel guilty about skipping school.

FRIDAY, MAY 27   I gained all my weight for the week and got my pass. Since I refused to go to school anymore, Vanessa and I planned a big shopping trip. We were getting ready to go when Sheena, the head nurse, called me from her office to wait. I could tell she was talking to the schoolteacher on the phone because she couldn't get a word in edgewise and kept rolling her eyes. They talked for about half an hour while I waited outside, chewing my fingernails. I was pretty scared because I've never been in trouble like that before. Chris was there too, and she was furious at the scandal. "You always exaggerate," she said. "You don't tell things like they are. And you and your Mom have a little thing going. Every time something bad happens, you run to your Mom to fix it!"

I couldn't help crying a little, although I fought it. My voice was shaking as I told Sheena my side of the story, and I felt ashamed. She was quite nice to me but said I need to stand on my own two feet. I said, "I tried to. I made an important decision on my own and

I tried to stick with it." She patiently explained that I must accept opposition to my decisions, think them through, and perhaps change my mind.

Around eleven Sheena and I had to go talk with the teacher. Apparently she had been almost hysterical with rage. As we walked up to the classroom, I thought, "Forget it, lady. I'm not going to let you terrify me!" When we got there, she was sugar sweet. "Hiiii," she said with a false smile. "Nice to seeee you. Let's go to the quiet room, OK?"

I had to apologize. "I'd like to apologize for walking out of the class." (I did *not* apologize for anything I said.) "I felt I was justified at the time, but perhaps I acted too quickly."

She accepted my apology and then went on with a half-hour-long prepared speech explaining her position and expectations. I tried not to yawn. Sheena bawled me out on the way back to the ward for not saying simply, "I apologize for my behavior." I was glad to have the crisis over but still refused to go to school for the rest of the day.

Vanessa and I had fun shopping but didn't buy much. Pacific Centre always impresses me — it's so huge. I consider it one of the modern wonders of the world — but then my mind is easily boggled. We came back around four o'clock, exhausted but happy. We played Trivial Pursuit and then went for supper. Vanessa didn't even watch my plate like she used to. She just ate. I ate pretty well too. I'm slowly getting used to it. And meals usually take only half an hour to eat now.

After supper, I was putting my cafeteria card back in my purse, when I saw my little container of sunflower seeds and nuts. I always keep them handy in case I get a low-blood-sugar attack. It looked different, somehow, so I took off the lid. The container was empty. Vanessa had eaten every last bit. At first I was hurt and angry that she would go into my purse and take something that was mine. Then I remembered something Mom said to us as a joke: "You can't get much lower than stealing an anorexic's food." I knew she must feel just awful, so I didn't say anything. If she would pick the lock on a freezer that belonged to the people she was staying with, she'd certainly eat my sunflower seeds.

Unfortunately, Samantha is back in the hospital, on the acute wing. She's only been out of here for two weeks, but I guess her binging got pretty bad. She's on an i.v., and her ECG showed severe heart malfunction. She's really playing with her life. My heart goes out to her.

SATURDAY, MAY 28   Vanessa was pretty excited this morning because her dad was coming. She kept asking, "Are you sure I don't look fat? I want to look my best." She was, of course, gorgeous, and she knew it. But her parents put a lot of emphasis on her looks. The first thing her father said was, "Vanessa, you look great." And her mother sent a card that said, "I know you can do it. Beauty is just around the corner." I think this makes Vanessa feel that her looks are the most important thing about her. What would her parents do if she were disfigured in a terrible accident? Would they still love her?

SUNDAY NIGHT, MAY 29   I had a great weekend. I didn't lose any weight while I was at my aunt's, and I walked around outside quite a lot and got a sunburn.

Back on the ward, Vanessa was as red as I and very happy. She had done very well all weekend and was ending her eleventh day of no binging and no vomiting. She was floating on air. I gave her a hug because we were happy.

FRIDAY, JUNE 3   Today is less gray and cloudy than it has been. Hints of blue are appearing in the sky, and the air is pleasantly cool. I weighed in at 0.1 kg less than I'm supposed to be for my pass, but Chris decided that the 4:00 weigh-in is what really counts. I'm sure that by then I'll be at least 37.4 kg (82.5 pounds) and I'll be able to go. I can't wait to see Dad—he's coming today and it's been months since I've seen him. I'm also invited to friends' for supper. This weekend is going to be great. I don't want to go to school today because the day already has that weekend atmosphere, even though it's only Friday morning.

Karen hates her body. She has a humpback now because when she was eleven and just starting to develop she hunched over to hide her breasts. She thinks breasts are dirty and disgusting. She finally agreed to take a shower. This is hard for her because although she has an obsession with cleanliness, she can't stand to look at her body. Going to the bathroom is a big ordeal that requires at least an hour of washing afterwards.

I didn't have to go to school this afternoon, and it was great. Vanessa and I were both in an odd mood, and I started a pillow fight. We laughed so hard our guts ached. Vanessa rolled right off the bed! At one point when she whipped the pillow at me the pillowcase stayed in her hand and the pillow went zinging across the room, hit my plant, and knocked it over. We were both so hysterical with laughter that the staff kept looking in at us.

"That's not allowed, you know," Sheena said.

"What, pillow fights?" I asked.

"No, having fun," she answered.

After that we settled down a bit and Vanessa gave me a complete makeover. She French-braided my hair, and I put on my white shoes, white skirt, and a matching white blouse. No one could believe it was me! The other patients all freaked out because I finally looked my age. Everyone complimented me, and I felt so happy and full of energy. The only problem was that I was starting to feel fat. My stomach is huge — it's a real potbelly. The rest of me is staying skinny and my gut is growing rounder every day. I wish I could take some flesh off it and put it on my shoulders and back. I feel like a marshmallow supported by two toothpicks.

7:00 P.M. I can't believe it. My makeup is dissolved in tears. My beautiful white outfit is stained with mascara because I've been crying into my lap. The scale says I've lost 0.4 kg, or almost a pound, since 7:00 this morning. I'm numb. No more cafeteria, no more school, no visitors, no leaving the ward. I won't even get to see my dad. It hurts so much, I can't even cry anymore. I don't understand how it happened! I guess it must have been that fruit salad I ate at lunch. It just wasn't enough. I must have been subconsciously cutting down because I felt fat.

Kim tried to comfort me; she's a good friend. But she, like everyone else, gets to go out for the weekend. I had to phone my friends to tell them I can't come for dinner. They were so disappointed! I told Mom I'm leaving, running away if I have to. But I guess I didn't really mean that, and she knew it. She told me to act seventeen. So I changed my clothes, washed my face, and tried to eat even more. I sobbed and studied the evening away. The fat, ugly nurse is on tonight. I asked her if there were any possibility of my getting out just for an hour or so. She turned her fat face to me, pursed her lips in a prissy way, and practically yelled, "Absolutely not!"

I was sitting on a chair out in the hallway when Marnie, the little Jamaican woman, sat down beside me. "What's the matter?" she asked. I told her about losing all my privileges and not even being able to see my dad. When I looked at her, tears were rolling down my face. "I feel for you," she said. I gave her a hug.

SATURDAY, JUNE 4 Today has been very lonely. There are about three of us on the ward. I feel stronger and better able to cope with being here now that I've had a good night's sleep. I wish I'd quit waking up so early, though. It's one of the symptoms of anorexia nervosa. I did homework and studying, but mostly I just ate. When I'm not busy, and have more time to think, I get more depressed.

Now that I'm eating so much and have given up so many of my anorexic ways, I feel as if a part of me is gone. I'm not Maureen the skeleton anymore; I'm Maureen the person. It's scary because I don't know how to be a grown-up person. I know how to be a child and how to be an anorexic, but I've never really been a teenager. I'm scared to see what Maureen the person will do with her life.

Sometimes I miss that security that comes with not eating. I can stay in my own narrow world and know that I can withstand deprivation and want. I can be sure that if I ever needed to, I could go without.

My body continues to develop and sometimes I'm glad, but sometimes I'm scared. I watched Kim eating supper today and it was like looking in a mirror. She did exactly the same things that I was doing two months ago. She sits alone on one of the couches (we are not allowed to eat in our rooms on this ward) and puts her tray on the coffee table. She takes out her napkin and puts it on her lap. Then she separates all the food items so that no two are touching. She divides each item in half or quarters, or however much she has decided to eat that day. Then she begins the long, slow process of transporting tiny amounts of food from tray to mouth. It takes about an hour. Watching her upset me because instead of feeling glad that I'm not like that anymore, I wanted to say, "Hey, I was sick too! I had a hard time eating! I don't really want to eat this. I promise I'm not really enjoying it." It doesn't make sense, and I feel ashamed for thinking that way.

The day dragged on forever. Vanessa got home early, but I was too tired to talk much.

SUNDAY, JUNE 5 I have gained a measly 0.3 kg, or 0.66 pound. Today was long and boring, but I was permitted to see Mom and Dad from 11:00 to 1:00. We played Trivial Pursuit, and they both loved it. Dad looks good, but a bit strained and tired. Sometimes they both look old to me. That scares me. I want them to stay young and healthy—not for my sake, but for theirs. I know that Mom has aged a lot during the last year and a half. Sometimes I notice crow's feet around her eyes.

Four dollars and a bag of cookies were stolen from my room today. At first I thought Vanessa took the cookies, but she said no and I believe her. And she has enough money; why would she need mine? I do know that she's been in my purse before, though, and she opens my drawers when I'm not here. Anything she finds, she eats. Then she feels bad and tells me or buys me something else. "I didn't do it!" is her first reaction whenever something goes wrong.

MONDAY, JUNE 6 Well, I'm alone for a whole month. Mom and Dad left tonight. It was a happy goodbye, though, and I know I can handle being alone just fine. I got all my privileges back and even got to go out for an evening pass. We drove through Chinatown and then had a dinner at the Spaghetti Factory in Gastown. My biggest fear confronted. I didn't eat all my spaghetti, but then who could? I ate quite a bit, and I didn't even get upset at seeing all that food on my plate.

It sure felt good to eat without all that terrible guilt, fear, anxiety, and frustration. I was pretty proud of myself, and I think Mom and Dad were proud of me too. It felt so different. I felt free and lively. I wasn't secretly estimating calories or thinking ahead about how I could compensate the next day. I was actually enjoying the meal. It was a pleasure, not a terror.

Life without anorexia can be OK. It's going to be hard to go back into the real world, but I want to. I'm excited—I can't believe how much I've grown up and how excited I am about my life.

TUESDAY, JUNE 7 What a bore this place is. I want to get out and start doing things again. I've been living in my isolated little anorexic world for three years. It's time to get moving.

We had a really good group therapy meeting today. The room was just packed full of people. More and more women are developing anorexia nervosa. Our society has a complete preoccupation

104

with thinness. As Dr. Sandor says, the image we all have of the "perfect" body is one that is not very healthy. But we are made to believe it's the only acceptable way to be. We are not normal if we have a layer of fat on our stomachs.

Now there are three women in their late thirties or early forties in the group. This is really an epidemic! There's even a song about anorexia, called "Anna-wrecks-ya."

Somehow we got onto the subject of anger. I said I thought anger was a negative thing, a sign of weakness. When I was younger, I used to lose my temper and yell at my sister or my friends. But when I was older and had developed a strong conscience, I grew to hate this in myself. I decided to change and to discipline myself. I respected my mother very much because even when she was provoked she never lost her cool.

We discussed the idea of anger as negative and decided that there are productive and destructive ways of expressing anger. It doesn't have to be expressed by losing your temper. Dr. Sandor says it's important not to always be so passive, that you shouldn't deny the existence of anger within you. He says that anger should be vented in some productive way and that depression is anger turned inward.

I think this is true. There are a few people to whom I should have expressed my anger, but instead I just cried. I have to learn how to calmly and firmly show that I am not pleased. But I know it's going to take time.

Dr. Sandor also said that I must do things that don't necessarily improve my intellect. I don't have to do everything for the sake of productivity and accomplishment. I have to learn to stop and smell the roses instead of reading *The Complete Grower's Guide to Fragrant Flowers*.

WEDNESDAY, JUNE 8   My weight suddenly jumped up seven points today. I have to admit that it was pretty scary to find it had gone up so much. I guess the weight has accumulated over the last few days and finally showed significantly today. I didn't eat as much yesterday, so who knows how my crazy body works? I guess I am subconsciously slowing a bit, taking in fewer calories. But I'm still trying and still determined to get out of here by June 26. I suppose I will always have to fight back those feelings that now I'm inferior to the way I used to be.

Today I feel kind of hurt. It's a little thing, really, and I tried to ignore it. But it feels as if there's a big hole in my stomach. I've put up with a lot from Vanessa and never held anything against her. I've let her steal my food, go through my purse, make fun of my religion, and tell me off in front of others. But now she's down in the dumps because she's going home tomorrow and she binged all day today. When I try to talk to her and comfort her, she just bites my head off. "You wouldn't understand!" she screams. "Just leave me alone!"

I went to Dr. Sandor's office today to pick up an envelope I left there. He gave me a kiss, congratulated me, and said I was starting to look like a young woman. I can't believe it! I only have eight more pounds to go. I feel about fifteen, and I wish I were because all those early teen years were wasted. I wasn't alive. I mean, I was alive, but not living. When I look back, I can recognize depression. But at the time, I just thought that life was one continuous worry. Will I gain a pound? Should I gain a pound? Will I get an A? Things look brighter now.

It's hard to accept this new body that I'm developing every day. It's so substantial and so foreign. I can no longer decide how it's going to be. I must buy all new clothes and underwear. I'm happy, but I'm scared too. I can no longer hide in that tiny body. I have to learn to accept the life of an ordinary, normal person.

Karen the hand washer is making real progress. Her immersion treatment is starting to work already. The doctor and some nurses take her into a little room and rub their hands on the floor and the bottoms of their shoes. Then they put their "contaminated" hands on their faces, in their hair, and so on. Karen has to watch this. It's very hard for her to take, but it's working. This morning she put her shoes on without washing afterwards. That's quite an accomplishment for her. Her medication is making her so groggy that she walked right into a wall last night.

THURSDAY, JUNE 9   Well, Vanessa leaves today at 4:00. She sure is going out with a bang. She binged all day yesterday and then threw up several pounds of food. I was trying to encourage her not to barf before I went to school. She had eaten three lunches and was in a lot of pain. I guess I said the wrong thing and set her off. She started yelling and saying terrible things. She said that I am too suspicious of her and that I think I'm smart because I can eat more than her and not gain weight. She said my family smothers me and won't let me live my own life. "You'll never grow up," she said.

When I got back from school, Vanessa was nowhere to be seen. I cleaned up her mess in our room and made her bed—again—and felt a little better. I decided I would treat her as usual. Why deliberately make things uncomfortable? But when she didn't show up, I started getting worried. Had she continued to binge? Had she thrown up? It was really bothering me, although I knew it was none of my business. But I really care, and I felt that maybe I was partly to blame. Perhaps I said something wrong, and she'd gone out to slit her wrists. Then I came across something that practically made my heart stop. I opened one of her drawers to put a book away, and there was a rather familiar-looking yogurt container. Things had been going missing all day—some cheese and crackers, half a piece of cake that someone had given me, and some fruit. Countless things had "mysteriously" disappeared over the last few days. I knew that the yogurt container was mine and that Vanessa must have taken it and all the other things, including the four dollars out of my wallet. Later I casually mentioned that someone had taken my yogurt. Vanessa looked shocked and innocent. "Why that's terrible!" she said. "Who would do a thing like that?"

I felt stabbed. "I don't know," I said.

What a convincing liar. She really had me believing that she was innocent. Bulimics are artists at deception. But did our friendship mean so little to her? Just before she left tonight I confronted her. "I want you to know that I know everything and it's OK. I'm sorry for tempting you."

She just looked at me. Her face didn't even redden. "Thanks" was all she said.

I said, "Did you take the money too?"

"Yes," she answered.

Later Diane told me I was a jellyfish whom no one would ever respect because I can't stand up for myself. Nice people can't get along in this world, she said. This episode reminded me of when I was "friends" with Jane Carter in grade four. She treated me like a slave, like absolute dirt. And I took it because I thought I needed her help in arithmetic. I was too insecure to try it on my own. I must be a supple jellyfish that immediately molds to each new person, situation, and expectation. I am *not* a concrete person.

Anyway, it was very hard to see Vanessa go. I helped her pack, waited with her, comforted her, encouraged her. I had bought a Garfield card and got everyone on the ward to sign it. She was thrilled. When she left we hugged, and then I waved until the car was out of sight. I felt empty and sad. I decided to phone Dad, and he cheered me up.

FRIDAY, JUNE 10 Joanne, a severely anorexic woman, has taken Vanessa's place on C-1. She arrived around ten last night. She weighs eighty-nine pounds and is five foot six. She has a bad heart and huge pockets of edema on her ankles and under her eyes. She's lost almost all her hair.

I got talking to her. She unpacked her things while I lay in bed and tried to stay awake. Joanne is a painter, and her paintings sell for eight hundred to a thousand dollars each. The deal is that she must gain one pound per week, and, if she doesn't make it, she must give the hospital one painting each time she misses.

"I'd love to see your work," I said. She handed me some slides. I held them up to the light and complimented her on them. They were splashes of different colors, each one huge enough to take up nearly a whole wall. A particularly large pink one attracted my attention.

"What's this one?" I asked.

"Oh, they're all pictures of the vagina," she answered. "It's sort of my symbol."

"Oh, how nice," I said.

Joanne is twenty-seven. She had been working at a Calgary art gallery until she got to the point where she could barely get up in the morning. Her dad finally convinced her to come to Vancouver for help. She is supposed to have a show in less than a year's time, and she hasn't even started yet. She's going to try doing a collection of sketches about her experience here. She's a severe insomniac, but at least she doesn't snore. I like her.

I gained a whole kilogram last night, so now I weigh 88.4 pounds. That means I have only 7 pounds to go, and I may be out of here in one and a half to two weeks. I'm really pushing. It's terrifying yet exciting at the same time. I don't feel fat, but I do feel more solid and a little less fragile. I think and concentrate much better, and I feel much happier and more optimistic about life in general.

I only went to school in the morning. After lunch, I went down to

King Edward Mall and bought a few things. I was put on level five yesterday, and it feels good to come and go whenever I want.

SATURDAY, JUNE 11   Today I felt fat and ugly, and I really had to force myself to eat. My stomach is a large pot, and I'm still pretty skinny everywhere else. The nurses say that this is to be expected and that it will take about six months for the weight to distribute evenly. I've still got a little girl's body, but Chris says I look really good. I feel great except that I'm such a funny shape, I can't find any clothes to fit.

I'll just have to wait it out, I suppose. Sally, my friend from group therapy, says it took her two years to completely recover and get back a normal body. I guess I won't get better overnight. Dr. Sandor says I must not think I'm fat, because I'm still way underweight.

MONDAY, JUNE 13   The start of another long, boring week. I'm getting so restless to get out of here. I went to school, studied a bit, and then spent the afternoon lying around trying not to burn up any calories. Around four I got a roomful of visitors—five teenagers. DaleAnn met a guy named Roger in Saskatoon. When he moved to Vancouver she asked him to visit me. He arrived with three friends, and Sally also happened to be here.

Since I didn't like my hard mattress, they helped me trade mattresses with the spare bed. It was hilarious! The four guys liked Sally and me, and we really liked them. We had a great time. I was totally shocked to see that I could handle the situation just fine. I wasn't stuck for words or worrying about the studying I wasn't getting done. I was actually having fun with kids my own age!

After they all left, Sally and I went for supper at the cafeteria and then goofed around all night in my room. She stayed until way after visiting hours were over.

TUESDAY, JUNE 14   I wrote my social studies final today. I was all worked up and nervous. I wrote it in the quiet room, but the teacher kept coming in and saying, "How are we doing?" I wished she would get lost, but she kept giving me tips on how to write exams. She went on and on until I could have screamed.

THURSDAY, JUNE 16   School today was a joke. A girl my age from Children's named Tanya and I were the only ones there. The teacher whisked Tanya off to the quiet room (what a dumb name) to practice her typing. "Don't peek," the teacher chirped, "or I'll give you forty lashes with a long wet noodle—ahehee! Haaa!"

I attempted a feeble smile just so the hag wouldn't feel too bad. She's a jerk, yes, but I can't stand to be deliberately cruel to anyone. Tanya didn't smile. She never does. She hardly ever says a word or puts an expression on her face. Tanya was in for a week or so about a month and a half ago. There didn't appear to be anything wrong with her, but she definitely was not a happy girl. Now she's back. The first day she came to school this time, the teacher gave me a little speech: "Now I want you to accept this girl. Be nice to her." Tanya came in, said nothing, and rolled her eyes at everything. The teacher deserves that treatment, though. She doesn't really care about the students. Tanya is just another "youngster" for her mark book.

Anyway, after Tanya came back from the quiet room, I was supposed to be writing and Tanya studying. But every time the teacher left the room, we'd start talking. After I carried the conversation for a while and showed her that I was her friend and not a nosy nurse, she began to open up. I think she needs to talk to someone her own age.

Tanya had a big bulky bandage on her left arm, so I asked her what happened.

"I fell out of the bathtub," she said.

"Oh," I said, "it must be quite bad."

"Yes, I really banged it," she said.

We started talking about how awful it was being in the hospital. I said that it was better on our new ward but that A-3 had been pretty depressing. Then Tanya opened up to me at last. "That's what I'm here for," she said, "depression."

I didn't want to probe, but I wanted her to know I cared and was concerned. After we shared our feelings of disgust for the teacher and her moldy jokes, Tanya started talking a little about her family. I asked if there had been some recent disturbances in her life to cause this depression. She said there had, but she didn't go into detail. Her mother and father are divorced, and she lives with her father. She's been in the hospital for two weeks. Her father has visited twice, her mother once. Her mother is getting remarried soon, and Tanya has only met her stepfather-to-be a few times.

110

She told me a few more sad things; then she thought for a moment. "I didn't fall in the bathtub," she said. "I did this to myself." She took off the bandage and revealed a huge greenish yellow bruise covering her whole arm from the elbow down.

"It's a lot better," she said. "It was all purple and swollen."

I cringed and gently touched the discolored skin. I wished I could do something that would make it stop hurting, just for a minute even.

"Why do you hurt yourself, Tanya?" I asked. "Are you trying to punish yourself?"

"I guess so," she said. She showed me five or six razor-blade cuts on her arms.

"How did you hurt your arm so badly?" I asked.

"I bashed it with a rock," she said.

We got to really talking and I was able to draw her out quite a bit. "You're the first one who has shown some real concern," she said. "Thank you." I could tell by her uncomplaining tone of voice that she wasn't just feeling sorry for herself. I told her that I'd come and visit this afternoon, and she seemed pleased.

Later I went to see her and we had a good talk. She has to run the house and look after her little sister all on her own. She feels alone and guilty constantly. It broke my heart when she told me about her suicide attempt. The doctors are really trying to help her, but Tanya's problem is that she's far too smart. She can see right through any façade. She can see through adults, and she doesn't respect them. I don't blame her—no one's given her any reason for her to respect them. She's a lot more adult than her parents or any other adults she's been in contact with.

FRIDAY, JUNE 17   Chris told me that the head nurse of Tanya's ward said I can't see her anymore in her room. If we want to visit, we must meet in the teen lounge and our visits must be timed. Tanya can only have two visitors a day.

We were sitting in the teen lounge talking today, really talking about ourselves and our problems. Suddenly, some kind of psych nurse or social worker came in. Of course Tanya immediately clammed up. The nurse tried to talk, but the conversation became stilted and phony. I wished the nurse would go away. Sometimes the nurses just try too hard. It's sickening. The phone rang, and

111

while the nurse was answering it, Tanya and I used the opportunity to sneak off to the children's playroom. Soon it was time for Tanya to go talk with her doctor. I promised to come again, and she was pleased, I could tell.

The rest of the day was boring. I did some math in school and then came back to the ward. In the evening Sally picked me up (she just got her license), and we went to a movie. She's just super!

SATURDAY, JUNE 18 Today Sally and I caught a bus down to the mall. At noon we had Greek food. I got brave and had chicken with rice. I was kind of scared afterward, but I calmed down by telling myself I could just have a salad for supper.

After lunch, we hit the stores. I was frustrated to find that I am right between girls' and women's sizes. I still have a little girl's figure, but I'm taller and larger than a little girl. Even some size three pants bag on me. It's upsetting, but neat in a way. I feel much more normal worrying about my shape and weight than walking around looking like a skeleton, pale as a sheet and thinking only of calories and punishment. Anyway, we walked around from 12:30 to 5:00, and by the time we went out to the bus stop my feet ached like they've never ached before. Talk about pain! I'm used to just sitting around in the hospital all day—I sure am out of shape.

SUNDAY, JUNE 19 Today I went to a friend's house for lunch. I was terrified! This was the first meal I had eaten in someone's home (besides Auntie Peggy's) since I came here. It was pretty upsetting, but I stayed fairly calm. I ate all the sandwiches and cookies that I was given, and I didn't even try to scrape off the butter.

I got back to the hospital around 3:30. At 4:30 I was playing Trivial Pursuit with Joanne when the phone rang. It was Terry, one of the guys I met when Roger and his friends came. He invited me to a baseball game that some kids were having. My immediate reaction was "No! I can't do that!" Then I thought, "Why not? Why on earth not? It's about time I started going out and having some fun!" All this thinking took a split second. I said, "Sure, I'd love to." He picked me up at 7:00, and I had a great time.

MONDAY, JUNE 20 Today went OK. I started my stomach-flattening exercises and did a half-hour on the exercise bike. I'm ninety pounds now, and I've reached a plateau—by choice. I made it over eighty-

112

five, but now I'm scared to gain any more. I think I look just fine, maybe even a bit chubby. I feel as if Dr. Sandor is trying to make me fat because he refuses to let me go before I'm exactly ninety-five pounds.

This morning I was wearing some yellow pants and a yellow T-shirt, and the pants were a little snug around my waist and abdomen area because that's where most of my weight has gone. Diane says that's because many of the vital organs are in the stomach area and must be protected by fat layers. They all say that my weight will redistribute itself if I'm patient and don't lose any weight. Anyway I felt really fat this morning and kept running to Diane for consolation and encouragement. She always makes me feel better, even though she sometimes talks roughly and is abrupt.

I went to visit Tanya in the afternoon. She was glad to see me. The girl in the bed next to her is fifteen and is in for the third time for the same problem—VD. Tanya says she "has an infection."

When I came back to the ward, some creepy guy named Melvin was waiting for me. He heard through some of Roger and Terry's friends that I was in the hospital and has visited me several times. I call him Melvin the Mouse.

"Oh no," I whispered as he approached. He said he'd been waiting for an hour and a half and presented me with pink rose buds. I thanked him and went to the kitchen to find a vase. Melvin followed.

"I see you've gained a lot of weight around the midriff," he said.

After Melvin left, I burst into tears. Joanne tried to comfort me, but what was said, was said. I put on a baggy dress and went to the cafeteria, planning to have a salad. But when I got there, I just stood and looked at the food. I wanted to go home so badly! I wanted to be normal and happy. Then I looked at my arms and saw nice rounded flesh, not bones that protruded and felt like knife blades. So I had a cabbage roll and rice. When I finished, Kim took me for a ride in her car. We walked to her apartment and then drove down to Kits Beach and walked around on the sand. I felt quite a bit better and was glad to have missed the ward meeting. I still feel pretty rotund, however. I phoned Mom and cried a bit. I guess I'm still a real Mommy's girl.

TUESDAY, JUNE 21   I did my exercises and half an hour on the bike again. It feels good to exercise. Then I went off to school and suffered through the teacher's superiority, quirks, and snobbery. I had planned to wear my baggy dress again, but Joanne talked me out of it. I also told Diane about the incident with Melvin last night. She made me feel better. "Am I fatter than the normal person?" I asked. She told me that there is no "normal," that everyone is different. Fashion magazines try to set the norm, but half of the models don't even menstruate.

In the afternoon I went up to see Tanya again. The nurses wouldn't let her off the ward, so we sat outside and talked. I asked her what she talked to her social worker about.

She said, "Well, if you promise not to breathe a word of it to anyone — we talk about abuse. When I was eight I was abused — sexually."

My heart leapt, and I took her hand and closed my eyes. I kept thinking, "It's not fair, it's just not fair!"

"It was my brother," she said. "He's twenty-five now. I hate him."

I wanted to take that all away from her, to make it not have happened. We talked about it a little more. She said that now she can't even stand to have anyone touch her. She hasn't kissed her dad for over a year and a half. If someone brushes past her, she cringes. Poor Tanya. No wonder she's depressed.

WEDNESDAY, JUNE 22 A new patient named Donald arrived over the weekend. He's an old English guy. Every time he sees me, he says, "Anna should be here any minute. I want you to meet Anna." That's his daughter. Anyway, Diane told me to stay away from him because he's manic-depressive. He'll be fine and then suddenly he'll go into a tremendous rage.

Today while everyone was eating supper, Donald got really upset because he had to wear the hospital's pajamas for a few days until he was allowed to wear ordinary clothes. First he took his top off and walked around looking ugly. His pajama pants were falling off, and I was embarrassed for him and for everyone else. I said, "Uh, Donald, your, um, pants are falling down." He started cursing and yelling obscenities at the nurses for making him wear "these bloody pajamas." Then he ran to the nurses' station, took off his pants, ripped them to shreds, and threw them at a nurse. After that he came back to the eating area in his dirty, baggy underwear, sat down, bummed a smoke off Joanne, and began to settle down a bit.

114

THURSDAY, JUNE 23   I went swimming today with Joanne and Kim and Chris. The pool is fairly small but beautifully warm. Special pipes spurt warm jets of water to massage the body. It's great! The pool is used mostly for physiotherapy. We swam around and relaxed in big black inner tubes.

Then I went back to the ward and did my exercises and half an hour on the stationary bike. I felt great. After that I washed my hair and had my snack with Joanne — then wrote a poem and had lunch.

After lunch, I did some schoolwork and went to occupational therapy. The therapists kicked me out, though, because they don't accept any of Dr. Sandor's patients. Dr. Sandor has his own methods of treatment. These occupational therapists sure are nice. It was like a big family in the OT room. The patients give each other back rubs, exchange recipes, and talk about their problems.

I went to see Tanya. She bashed up her arms again and was getting casts on them when I came in. We sat down to talk, and when I sat down a little too close to her, she got up and moved. My heart just aches for her. She never complains or dramatizes the things that are happening to her.

Tanya has to act as mother figure to her brothers and sisters when she needs a mother herself. Neither her parents nor her other brothers and sisters know that she was sexually abused. They didn't even know that she had cut herself or attempted suicide. I'm going to see her every day for sure.

I choked down my supper — chicken teriyaki, rice, corn, chocolate milk, ice cream. It was a real struggle to get it all down.

FRIDAY, JUNE 24   I made my weekly goal weight with two points to spare. But poor Joanne! She was half a point off her goal weight. Now she loses a thousand-dollar painting and is confined to the ward. It just doesn't seem fair.

MONDAY, JUNE 27   Today is the worst day I've had in ages. From start to end it was bad, bad, bad. I'm hot, thirsty, and irritable even as I sit here. To start with, I had Bettina, the singing French twit, for my nurse. I was feeling pretty touchy, because I had just finished a huge breakfast (I have to gain three pounds in three days). Bettina came into my room and said, "I need to tell you something for the good of your health."

115

I rolled my eyes. "What am I in for now?" I thought. "I don't need her advice today."

She lay down on my bed and started showing me an exercise that would flatten my stomach. I couldn't believe it. It was as if she were saying, "You are too fat—exercise."

Tears streaming down my face, I ran out of the room. I had to talk to someone. I went to the lounge, where Joanne was working out on the stationary bike. She was very understanding, but what has been said can't be taken away. That is the second person who has noticed my big stomach! She couldn't have said a worse thing at a worse time. How could anyone be so tactless? Doesn't she know anything about anorexia nervosa?

At 9:30 I went to UBC with a psychology student for a test. She put me into the psychophysiotherapy laboratory, which was a soundproof, tiny gray room.

The purpose of the test was to measure my anxiety level when I was confronted with food. A Snickers chocolate bar was to be given to me, but I couldn't see it. I was hooked up to electrodes, which would measure my heart rate, breathing level, skin conductivity, blood flow, sweatiness, and so on—all indicators of anxiety. The electrodes were stuck on my forehead, chest, stomach, leg, and the fingers and thumb of one hand. After the electrodes had been checked, I was given a set of headphones and a microphone in order to communicate with the student.

The doors were closed, and I was left alone in ominous silence. The room was full of electrocardiogram equipment for graphing the pattern of heart contraction. There was also a video machine staring right at me. I stuck my tongue out at it. I was afraid to move a muscle in case the electrodes fell off. On my lap I held a clipboard with questionnaires and a pencil. There was a pause of about five minutes, and the woman instructed me to fill out a questionnaire about how I felt at that moment. I knew that I would be asked to eat later on, and that knowledge influenced my answers.

I had to rate my feelings of satisfaction, tension, and so forth on a scale of one to nine. When I finished that, there was another pause of about five minutes. Then I was asked to fill out another sheet exactly the same as the first. I also had to write down my most prominent thought. After another pause, I had to look at ten landscape paintings, one at a time, and record how much I liked each one — again on a scale of one to nine. This was a control against which to compare my reaction to eating the food. After that, I filled out the same questionnaire a third time. Then I was asked to eat a Snickers candy bar. I managed only one bite. I knew I needed the calories, but Bettina's words kept coming into my mind, and that was the best I could do. After that, I filled out two more sheets, with a five-minute pause between to indicate how I felt at that moment.

Finally, the doors were opened and the electrodes removed, and I was shown various readings. It was neat to see them. There was a marked increase in anxiety each time I spoke into the microphone and when I began to eat.

Back at the hospital, I had to fill out some more forms. The student is going to send me a summary of her findings in the fall.

I have to eat lots and lots today to make my goal by Thursday morning. I'm keeping the exercise down and the eating up. It sure is hard. I feel so short and stocky. My legs feel like huge mounds of flesh. It's awful. Joanne tells me that Bettina figures I should grow up and learn to accept things like what she told me. I think she should learn about anorexia nervosa — and tact! She gave Kim, Joanne, and Karen a bad time too.

Donald is really acting up again. He has to have one-on-one nursing. Everybody is terrified of him. He's so drugged up that he can barely see where he's going but insists on staggering around. He wonders off, going into any room but his own and getting upset when he doesn't find his belongings there. Finally the male nurse put a huge sign on his door saying DONALD. Fortunately, Donald has a private room.

Today I caught him squatting on the floor, trying very hard to pick something up. "But, Donald, there's nothing there," I said. "Let me help you up."

"Ah, this blasted place! Give me my bloody clothes, you arses!"

I left. Everyone tries to conceal a smile when he starts ranting and raving. The general attitude is "Oh, it's just Donald."

Diane says, "He *probably* won't hurt you. Just stay out of his way." This ranting, cursing, and throwing of objects goes on well into the night. Ah, the joys of life in a nuthouse.

I was feeling pretty good around two o'clock, so I decided to phone Mom. She sounded quite underwhelmed. I think she was upset or had been fighting with Dad or something. Anyway, something as little as that sent me into a crying spell followed by depression. I guess I'm afraid to leave the safety of C-1 and go back into the real world. Sometimes it seems so big and so hard that I'm not at all sure I can handle it. My symptoms of anorexia nervosa are lessening (I'm almost a normal weight, I sleep well, and I eat like everyone else), but inside I'm still sick. I can see myself back in here in a year. Sometimes suicide seems quite appealing. I've always been one to take the easy way out. But I hate myself for even thinking of suicide and for knowing I'm too chicken to do it.

TUESDAY, JUNE 28   Today I went to relaxation group. Just about everybody on the ward was there. It was fantastic. By the end of the forty-five minutes I was really relaxed.

Later I went for a walk with Kim. I was feeling so fat and panicky. Poor Kim. I think she's had it with me. Complain, complain, complain. She gave me a beautiful card yesterday, and I could have just bawled. What a sweetheart. Just having met her makes being here worthwhile.

Donald was finally taken to Vancouver General Hospital. He's just too dangerous to be kept here.

I'm so excited about going home! But I'm scared too. One day at a time, Mo, one day at a time.

WEDNESDAY, JUNE 29   Today whipped by. The morning was slow because I was so excited and impatient about going home. I really had to eat and take it easy, so I didn't exercise. I have to gain almost a whole pound today in order to get out of here tomorrow.

In the morning I visited Tanya from eleven to twelve. The nurses wouldn't let her come to my room. But we did go out on the balcony, under close supervision.

This afternoon I went to the Army and Navy surplus store in New Westminster and didn't get back until 5:30. It was a real gas! It was actually fun to go shopping again. I didn't have to try on clothes that just hung all over my bones. I'm not saying I'm pleased with my figure — far from it. But it's much better than it used to be. Diane says that I look stocky and big in the ribcage because I've got the body of a thirteen-year-old. I've got to wait and develop. Great — I'll be "developing" when I'm twenty-five!

118

It's important for me not to lose any of this weight, or the changes will be delayed even longer. But I can't gain too much weight either or this whole thing will start all over again. I hope Mom and Dad understand this. I guess I can't really say I'm cured. I don't know if I ever will be.

When I got back, I had supper and Sally came in. She'd been working hard all day at Grace Hospital and was having a little rest before she went home. I had a great time talking and laughing my guts out with Joanne and Kim. Later on I had a good discussion with Diane. She says I've got to start telling Mom and Dad that I'm moving out and then do so. Because I'm afraid to be on my own, I really have to do it. Diane says I should move out fairly soon after I get out of school, or else I never will.

One thing I have learned here is that I don't have to try to do things or think the same way as Mom or my sister or anyone else. I've been told this all my life, but I have only accepted it lately. Now when I think of myself, I see me, Maureen. And when I think of Mom, I see Mom. I don't confuse the two anymore. Diane says I must never let this new-found independence slip away.

I had a chocolate bar, which shocked the socks off Joanne, and went to bed confident that I'll make my weight tomorrow.

THURSDAY, JUNE 30   I got up early and weighed in. I was *exactly* 43.1 kg, or ninety-five pounds, which is my discharge weight! Diane said last night that they would probably let me go even if I were a couple of points off. I crawled back into bed, numb with happiness. I had been scared last night that I wouldn't be able to keep this weight on for long. Diane says I'm too strong a person to end up back in here. That made me feel good. Maybe she's right. I've gone through so much, and I pulled through OK.

I frittered away the morning in a happy haze. I swam with Kim (and laughed my guts out when she put six inner tubes around her body), went to relaxation group, didn't eat my snack (ha, ha), rearranged my clothes in the suitcase, exercised, and had a shower.

In an hour I'll be at the Vancouver airport. The nurses are happy for me, I can tell. I have a large suitcase, full enough to burst, and a duffel bag with a broken zipper. There are also two black garbage bags full of odds and ends, which I'll have to store.

I'm nervous and fidgety. I've said goodbye to everyone and taken a whole roll of pictures. Strangely enough, I don't want to forget this place. I want to be able to tell people how it was, to say, "This is where I grew up."

I know I'm going to miss the people I've met here and the security of life in the hospital. But I also know that it's time to enter the real world, to catch up on what I've missed, and to enjoy what's to come. At last I feel that maybe I can do it.

MOTHER

It was a beautiful summer day when Maureen came home from the hospital. Dale and I stood by the window at the airport and watched her walk, alone, from the plane. She looked so proud of herself, so much healthier, much more substantial than she had when she left Cranbrook for Vancouver.

I had to keep reminding myself, "She's not cured. She just received a good boost along the road to recovery. She still has a long way to go."

Once we got home, it became obvious that Maureen was not going to maintain her discharge weight of ninety-five pounds. Within a few days she was down to ninety-two pounds. But her attitude and her eating habits were good, and we began to see that she did not intend to let her weight drop very low. Over the next few months she struggled up and down from ninety, at the lowest, to the occasional triumph of ninety-five pounds.

Dale and I felt optimistic about Maureen's future and were grateful for the progress she had made, but we found that it wasn't smooth sailing. There was an ugly scene when Dale caught Maureen ordering a diet pop at McDonald's. Another time Maureen became very upset after eating a large box of butterless popcorn at the movies. It took me quite a while to make her see how foolish she was being that evening.

There had been some encouraging changes in Maureen's thinking, however. She didn't watch over me anymore as I prepared the meals. Sometimes she expressed a bit of nervousness about something new, like Mexican food. But if I didn't insist that she eat it, and if she knew that she could eat something else if necessary, she was usually willing to at least try it. Often she was surprised to find she liked it. Then she would feel really proud of herself, adding to her confidence that she was getting better.

121

Although Maureen had trouble staying at ninety-five pounds and often complained about her "fat gut," she was quite a different girl from the one who went into the hospital. She had more self-confidence and even got her driver's license. She began to develop more independence as she bombed around town in the little Volkswagen Beetle Dale bought for her. She still got good marks in school, but she didn't drive herself the way she used to. Sometimes she would complain that she just couldn't get "into" studying like she had before. I would say, "Good! I'm glad to hear it. That was not a normal way to be. Now you are like the rest of us. You do well in school; that should be enough for you. You don't have to be the best."

After Maureen graduated from high school, Dale and I took her to Vancouver to see Dr. Sandor again. She hadn't seen him for almost a year, and we were anxious to have his professional assessment. She had been holding her weight at ninety-five pounds for a couple of months then and she was proud of herself.

But Dr. Sandor didn't give her any praise. He told her that it was time to get her weight up to one hundred pounds. Although Maureen was shocked and disappointed, she came to see his point. She still hadn't started her period, and Dr. Sandor thought that five more pounds might trigger the process.

While that has not yet proved true, those last five pounds leading up to one hundred pounds seem to have marked some kind of turning point. As she gained each pound over ninety-five Maureen would be only a little nervous for a day or so, and then she would accept her new weight. Along with that acceptance, Maureen has also come to really enjoy food for the first time since she became anorexic. It makes me feel really good when Maureen wanders into the kitchen as I'm preparing a meal, snitches some food off the plate, and says, "When's supper? I'm hungry. Mmmm, this is good." This may be a common occurrence in most families, but it's almost a miracle to me.

Other things have changed for Maureen as well. She is so much more relaxed and happy since she graduated from high school. Under the doctor's supervision, she is going to try to taper off her antidepressants. I'm not in a hurry to see her get off them. I think if she had to stay on them the rest of her life, it would be a small price to pay for a normal, happy life.

Maureen certainly looks different. At one hundred pounds, she looks more like a woman than a child for the first time in her life.

I've changed quite a bit too. As I look over the past few years, I realize that I've learned some valuable lessons. I no longer lie awake at night wondering what I did to make Maureen sick. I have accepted the fact that I may not be the supermother I once thought I was. I have realized that it is all right for me not to be perfect either. Maureen and I are both imperfect human beings, but we do love each other.

I have really come to appreciate my happy marriage. I think it has grown stronger through adversity. I have learned to value Dale's less emotional approach and realize that his love for Maureen helped him to keep his patience when his strongest desire was to force her to eat. I feel ashamed of myself when I think how eager I was to pin the blame for Maureen's illness on Dale and to label him dictatorial. In contrast, he never in any way made me feel that I was to blame.

I am also stronger than ever in my religious convictions. I don't know how I could have got through the past few years without my relationship with God. I now think that the training I received as a Christian to be loving and patient served to help Maureen and did not hinder her in any way. Styles of psychology change, but God's word remains. "Love never fails."

I was also fortunate to find a book called *Psychobattery: A Chronicle of Psychotherapeutic Abuse* by Therese Spitzer. It tells the stories of people who, already suffering the pain of having a mentally ill child, were accused, blamed, and persecuted by misguided members of the psychological priesthood. To my shame, I found that many of them held up their heads and refused to be intimidated, as I had been, by the prevailing theories of "parent bashing." Reading this book helped me to expiate most of the last traces of guilt I still carried. I can't say I never feel any guilt, but I am able to handle the occasional twinge that arises.

Another lesson I learned through Maureen's long illness was that it is difficult but rewarding to come face to face with one's own prejudice. If anyone had asked me whether there should be any shame attached to mental illness, I would have denied it vehemently. Yet I have to admit that one of the most difficult moments for me was asking directions to the psych ward in Shaughnessy Hospital. It wasn't easy to publicly declare that my child was mentally ill. I still don't find it easy, but at least I recognize my problem honestly.

As for anorexia nervosa itself, I've decided that the causes differ with the individual. It seems the development of the disease is like the making of a stew or soup — each time, the stew is made of similar ingredients, but in slightly different proportions. The personality of the anorexic herself is a basic ingredient. She is almost always perfectionistic and competitive. Of course she must have a great deal of self-control as well. There may well be a contribution by the family of the anorexic, but I've come to see this ingredient as less important than I originally believed it to be. I recently heard of an anorexic whose family background was the exact opposite of Maureen's. It was hard to believe that this family had the same problem. The girl had been a neglected child, had been made a ward of the court at four years of age, was sexually abused by her adoptive father at fourteen, and was finally put into a group home. She began to diet to avoid the teasing she received because of her weight problem. Where were her too loving, overprotective parents?

I think another important ingredient in the making of an anorexic is our contemporary idea of beauty. How many times have I taken a doughnut with the comment "I shouldn't, but..." or put whipped cream on top of my dessert with the remark "I'm going to be bad"? The concept that fat is bad and thin is good permeates our society. Of course Maureen is still exposed to these concepts and ideals, but most of the time she seems able to see them objectively and to decide that she hasn't got time for such artificial standards.

I'm very proud of my daughter Maureen. She has worked hard to overcome a severe, little-understood illness. And I'm proud of myself, too. Battle scarred I may be, but I think I came out of this experience a wiser person. I could be bitter, but I am not. I really don't blame anyone — not Maureen, not myself, not Dale. Maureen and I are probably as close and loving as any eighteen-year-old girl and her mother could be. We laugh together, we listen to one another, we share confidences.

I'm looking forward to the day, quite soon, when Dale and I will be alone together — but never really alone because we have two wonderful daughters. One of them used to be very sick, but she isn't anymore.

124

DAUGHTER

I am sitting on my bed, listening to Bruce Springsteen. The curtains are open, and I can see Mr. Andrews, the neighbor, raking leaves on his lawn. My room is not pure white anymore. I have splashes of color in various places: a bright red framed ballet poster, a yellow straw hat, an orange sunset quilt. I just came home from hiking with friends. Afterwards everyone went to McDonald's for a shake. I had one too. It was no big deal.

This morning, I weighed in at ninety-seven pounds. Dad will be reasonably pleased when I tell him tonight. He likes me to get weighed at the clinic once a week. This arrangement annoys me because it's a nuisance, and it's also degrading. (I'm like a thermometer—95.4 one day and 96.0 the next.) But I get weighed nonetheless because I feel I owe it to my dad after what I've put him through.

It's been a year and four months since I was released from Shaughnessy Hospital. My discharge weight was ninety-five pounds, but Dr. Sandor has recently informed me that I must gain five more. "You see," he explained, "you must have a certain percentage of body fat before the pituitary gland sends the message to begin menstruation." At first I didn't think another five pounds was even possible, let alone necessary. But I slowly came to realize that it was silly to settle for nearly normal when I could be completely normal. I keep reminding myself that normal doesn't necessarily mean average. A person can be normal and still be unique and interesting.

This last year has been a real challenge for me. I've had to work hard at keeping a reasonable attitude, and it hasn't been easy on me or on my family. People think that once an anorexic has gained a sufficient amount of weight and been released from hospital, she's cured. This isn't so. For me, the hardest part was just beginning. I wasn't sure how much I needed to eat in order to maintain my goal weight, and I was terrified to go over that weight.

I dropped five pounds right away and spent the rest of the year trying to put it back on. My parents were often disappointed when I voiced some of the fears that still plagued me. For example, if someone besides my mother cooked, I was afraid that person would add extra butter or oil to the recipe. I still shied away from fats of any kind. I still thought too much about food and liked to know ahead of time what I would be expected to eat. Although common sense told me that I should eat as everyone else did, the idea of not eating much still really appealed to me. And for the first few months I was back at home, I still had a need to accomplish important things all the time.

Mom and Dad insisted that they would not stop pushing me and monitoring my weight until I reached ninety-five pounds. I never went below ninety pounds, but I just couldn't force myself to gain enough to get back to ninety-five. I reasoned that if I weighed that much in the morning, I'd surely weigh ninety-seven or more at night. Some of the worst arguments I had with my parents occurred after I was released from the hospital. Because I was nearly at a normal weight, I greatly resented their continued interference in my life. It was not until my goal weight was increased to one hundred pounds that I was able to go past ninety-five.

I had rediscovered the pleasures of eating, but I still felt that I needed some form of self-discipline. I toyed with the idea of burning myself and even tried it once with a curling iron. But it hurt a lot, and I knew that I was not pleasing God by damaging one of his creations, so I stopped.

My parents still watch pretty closely to make sure I eat what they think is reasonable. Once Mom and Dad went away for the week-end, and I stayed at home by myself. I knew I could easily use the opportunity to lose a few pounds and eat as little as I wanted. But, to my surprise, I found I no longer wanted to restrict myself, or make myself suffer. I ate good food because I wanted to, and I enjoyed it. Since then, I've been by myself quite often. After all, I am eighteen now, and I have a car and some independence. I eat at restaurants and at my friends' homes. I'm still nervous about having lunch out, but all other meals are just fine. I feel secure in the knowledge that I could resist fattening things if I had to, but because I'm not overweight I don't have to resist.

My life has changed a great deal, and I feel like a new person. I finally got up the courage to tell Ian that I was not in love with him. One month later he stole a credit card, a Porsche, and a gun and took off down to California to meet Cyndi Lauper. He came back to Canada to spend several weekends in jail. He had almost finished his sentence when he repeated the whole thing again, this time "buying" a pair of one-thousand-dollar alligator shoes and living in a Hollywood penthouse. Since he was eighteen by then, the police didn't go so easy on him. I haven't seen him since.

I got my long hair cut off and people say I look much older now. And I took classes in school that I could really enjoy. I no longer feel guilty for enjoying what I eat. I've learned not to be scared if someone gives me a huge plate full of food. Now I can just eat the right amount for me and leave the rest. Before, I felt guilty just for having so much food in my possession. I never used to be able to eat food that was bunched together on a plate either. I needed it to be separated.

I don't need to take a long time to eat now. I don't savor each bite as if it were my last or cut my food into tiny bits. I've really expanded the range of foods I will eat. I'll try new foods now sometimes.

I'm still on antidepressants, but I think I'll be able to taper off them soon. I feel confident that I can live a healthy, happy life without them. My parents are less sure, but I am determined to show them I can do it. Occasionally I have the opportunity to talk to anorexic girls who are suffering through the same things I did. I tell them that if they are offered an antidepressant, they should take it and work with it, not against it. They should allow it to take away some of their fanatical concern about what they eat.

However, pills can't work miracles. Effort and determination are required, even after you have put on weight. Kim and Joanne haven't been as fortunate as I have. They were both released shortly after I was and have since been rehospitalized at dangerously low weights. This is Joanne's second hospitalization and Kim's seventh. Sometimes I think they are competing with each other to see who is more anorexic.

Perhaps Kim and Joanne haven't been able to keep their weight up because they achieved their normal weight by eating great quantities of low-calorie foods while retaining most of their food fears. For example, they drank skim milk, while I learned to drink whole milk. They ate only broiled chicken without skin, while I made myself eat fried chicken with the skin on. Although I suffered more psychologically by forcing myself to eat forbidden foods, they suffered physically because they had to eat an awful lot of salad and other low-calorie foods in order to gain weight. Neither really stopped her ridiculous exercising either.

I knew all through my hospital stay that I would be going back home and that Mom and Dad would expect me to eat normally. Also, I wanted to be able to eat like a normal person. Joanne and Kim knew they would be living on their own. They knew they only had to live up to their own expectations and could fool themselves into believing they were eating enough. Perhaps while I learned to overcome my fears, they just learned to live with theirs. I can understand their fears. Before I went into the hospital, I would always end up crying if someone tried to make me eat something I was afraid of. And a person who is in hysterics can't eat very easily — anorexic or not. But in Shaughnessy, I would try little bits of butter or milk or other foods that scared me and gradually work up to more. The pills helped tremendously, and after a while I could usually push aside my fears.

Now, as time passes, I think less and less about the food I eat and how I look. I am busy with other things, and I no longer have time for such a selfish preoccupation. Sometimes I worry about being fat or self-indulgent, but most of the time I maintain a realistic outlook. I try to concentrate on the spiritual, not the physical. I remember what Dr. Sandor always quoted: "Vanity, vanity; all is vanity." I also think of my nurse, Diane. She is a few pounds overweight, and yet she is happy. She has a career and a boyfriend and is a very "together" person. I admire and respect her. I'm not saying that I'll allow myself to get fat, but it wouldn't be the end of the world to be a little bit overweight.

I can see that each day I become less of an anorexic and more of a person. The battle keeps getting easier. I don't think about suicide anymore, but about life and a happy future. Occasionally I do some silly thing like drink a diet pop or pick the walnuts out of my maple walnut ice cream cone. But most of the time I'm reasonable, happy, and well fed. I feel grateful to have my anorexic days behind me, and I look forward to the future with confidence.